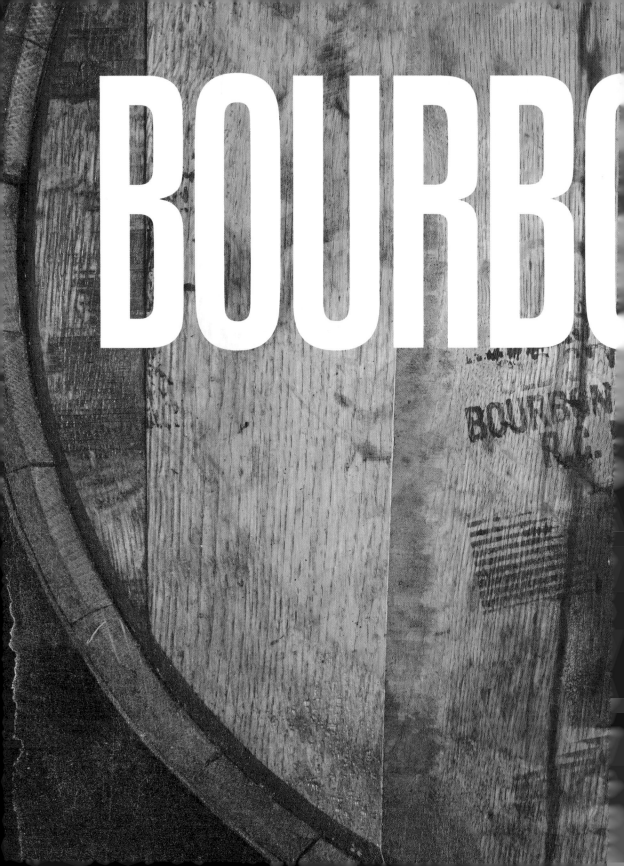

# N LAND

## A Spirited Love Letter to My Old Kentucky Whiskey

## EDWARD LEE

*Photographs by Jessica Ebelhar*

ARTISAN BOOKS | NEW YORK, NY

Library of Congress Cataloging-in-Publication Data is on file.

ISBN 978-1-64829-153-1

Cover design by Nina Simoneaux
Design by Headcase Design and Nina Simoneaux

Artisan books may be purchased in bulk for business, educational, or promotional use.
For information, please contact your local bookseller or the Hachette Book Group
Special Markets Department at special.markets@hbgusa.com.

The publisher is not responsible for websites (or their content)
that are not owned by the publisher.

The Hachette Speakers Bureau provides a wide range of authors for speaking events.
To find out more, go to hachettespeakersbureau.com or
email HachetteSpeakers@hbgusa.com.

Published by Artisan,
an imprint of Workman Publishing,
a division of Hachette Book Group, Inc.
1290 Avenue of the Americas
New York, NY 10104
artisanbooks.com

The Artisan name and logo are registered trademarks of Hachette Book Group, Inc.

Printed in China on responsibly sourced paper
First printing, February 2024

1 3 5 7 9 10 8 6 4 2

"I do not care to live in a world that is too good to be genial, too
ascetic to be honest, too proscriptive to be happy."
—HENRY WATTERSON

"All around me a voice was sounding:
This land was made for you and me."
—WOODY GUTHRIE

# CONTENTS

# INTRODUCTION

Every time I pour myself a glass of bourbon, I think about the passage of time. There is the time that has passed while the bourbon was aging in a barrel—four years, six years, eight years, and so on. With each passing year, the liquid maturing into a libation that is darker, more complex, more precious. There are trade secrets, family recipes, and knowledge passed on, history and traditions that stretch back for generations on a family tree through the hollers and hills of Kentucky. Their influence, their photos, their presence hovering over distilleries like ghosts passing through walls, forever linking the past to the lives of the people guiding bourbon into an uncertain future.

There is also the oak tree that goes into every barrel, which is the root of bourbon's flavor. It can take seventy to one hundred years for an acorn to transform from a seedling into the mature oak that winds up in the glass that I hold up to the sunlight fading outside my window. There are the countless hours and days and years of labor logged by the corn farmers, the rye and wheat farmers, the families that have devoted their lives to nurturing these isolated crops that will become bourbon. There are so many things that happen simultaneously and over time to culminate in this brown liquid that smells of tanned leather and burnt fruit and toasted hay and wet earth and dried spices. There is also the quick and fleeting passage of time, the phenomenon that happens over just minutes in a glass when the bourbon relaxes from a tight, locked concoction into a perfume that fills the room. The ice slowly melts and gives movement to the bourbon, allowing it to breathe and exhale its aromas. Bourbon is never static; it never occupies a single identity. It is mercurial and restless. It is a path into a part of our lives that remains dormant without it.

And bourbon is also about the measures of my own life. I think about how bourbon has played its role at every stage. The misspent youth drinking cheap bourbon and listening to the rebellious music that defined my teenage rage. When I was old enough to go to bars, how many long nights were spent in conversation as the hours evaporated into thin air, the music, the laughter. As I get older, I consume less and drink slower, sips instead of shots, slowing time to appreciate the craft and the nuances in every drink. And as a chef, I think about the transition I have made from consuming bourbon as a libation to using bourbon as an ingredient, a tool, a luxurious gift that enhances my craft.

For people outside Kentucky, bourbon may be considered a trendy drink, but in the Bluegrass State, bourbon is a way of life. It is our economy, our history, our livelihood, and our traditions. So as much as this book is a love letter to bourbon, it is by extension a love letter to Kentucky, a place that is my adopted home and one that I have embraced with an eagerness and joy I did not think I could possess. I found my culinary voice in Louisville. I met my wife here, and my daughter was born here. My flagship restaurant, 610 Magnolia in Louisville, is more than twenty-one years old and going strong. And for as long as I have been here, I have been cooking with bourbon in some form or another. These pages and these recipes are a culmination of that journey, colored with splashes of bourbon—a liquid that is more than just a drink poured over ice.

The magic that makes bourbon an irresistible libation is also what makes it an indispensable ingredient in my kitchen. The taste of bourbon is so distinctive, so strong, so haunting, that it makes my cooking instantly better. It gives recipes dimension and depth, layers and soul. It adds umami and smoke and caramel and tannins. To cook with bourbon is to respect it. It is a practice in balance and beauty. It requires no special education, but it demands your attention. It is the ultimate luxury ingredient but so readily accessible that it can seem mundane. The flavor of bourbon is many characteristics, but mostly it is time trapped in a bottle. Knowing how to cook with it becomes an obsession. In these pages, the places, the people, and the histories I write about are the result of a lifetime with bourbon at my side as a culinary companion.

# WHO IS BOURBON?

Bourbon is my best friend. I don't mean that in the way a person with a dependency might say it. It's a metaphor; a way to describe why I like bourbon over other spirits. Bourbon is like the easygoing friend who never complains about where you're going or how hot the car ride is. Bourbon doesn't argue with you much, and he is always good for a laugh. He is the friend you never tire of, even after you've heard all his jokes and know all his stories.

I have many "friends," and they all have a place in my universe. I love tequila and she is always ready for a late night at a moment's notice, but mysteriously, I always end up breaking the law when she's around. Gin and I have always had a contentious relationship. He shows up a little too well-dressed and perfumed and always has to be the center of attention. I love the thought of being his friend, but I feel like he is my companion out of pity, and he never lets me forget it. I dated vodka for a bit, but I hardly recognize her anymore, with all her candied lipsticks and ostentatious outfits. The few times that I do see her, she is more concerned with her selfies than she is about anything I have to say. Scotch is who I want to be when I grow up: an educated man with pedigree and charm, a Rhodes scholar who regales me with stories of faraway adventures and dinners at castles. I am giddy in his company, and when I am around him, I use phrases like "pardon me." But he and I both know that I will never be like him. Irish whiskey is bourbon's distant cousin, and while I like him very much, after a drink or two, I can't understand a word he is saying. I have many other international friends, like cognac and soju and grappa. I am happy to see them, but only when I'm visiting their home countries. I never write or call them otherwise. That makes me a horrible friend, but it's easier this way. Because I already have a best friend, and his name is bourbon. There have been times over the years when we've taken necessary breaks from each other to cool off. But sooner or later, we always seem to run back to each other and pick up right where we left off. There is never an awkward moment.

# BUT WHAT ABOUT WHISKEY?

What is the difference between bourbon and whiskey? There are a couple of facts to clarify for the uninitiated. Whiskey (or whisky, if you're from Scotland or Canada) is the broad term for almost any brown spirit made from grain. So bourbon falls under this category, but all whiskey is not bourbon. Here are the strict rules by which a distilled spirit can be called a bourbon. (If you already know this stuff, you can skip to page 18, but I hope you like reading about bourbon laws and its history—that's page 22—as much as I do.)

- Per the TTB (Alcohol and Tobacco Tax and Trade Bureau), in order to be classified as bourbon, a whiskey needs to be distilled from a fermented mixture of grains, or mash, that's at least 51 percent corn.

- Straight bourbon whiskey has to be aged for a minimum of two years, while bottled-in-bond bourbon must be aged for at least four years.

- Bourbon must be aged in new charred oak barrels—most distillers prefer wood from new white oak trees—and it cannot include any additives or colorings.

- While whiskey can be made anywhere in the world, it can be called "bourbon" only if it's made in the United States. This is due to legislation passed by Congress in 1964 that declared bourbon "America's Native Spirit."

- Bourbon also has proof requirements; it cannot enter the barrel at less than 80 proof or more than 125 proof. It also must be distilled at no higher than 160 proof.

# HOW BOURBON IS MADE

"I've never made a drop of whiskey in my life . . . we make bourbon in Kentucky, they make whiskey in Tennessee."
—JIMMY RUSSELL

The process of making bourbon is quite simple or quite complicated, depending on who you ask. It starts in the field with corn and ends in a distillery after years of aging. Before it gets to your glass, bourbon has passed through many hands, a staff of experts, and ultimately a restaurant/bar/shop owner who has selected that brand to feature. The following is a step-by-step process, but within each step is a world of science and know-how that has been handed down for generations.

**MASH BILL SELECTION.** A mash bill is a recipe of which grains will be used to create bourbon. The American Bourbon Association requires that bourbon sold in the United States be distilled from a mixture of grains composed of at least 51 percent corn. The remainder of the recipe is usually a combination of malted barley, wheat, or rye. This is the first important step in determining the flavor of a bourbon, and one that is carefully considered by the master distiller.

The first steps in the bourbon process take grains from mash to fermentation.

**MILLING AND MASHING**. Once the recipe has been determined, distilleries source the dried grains from various farms in the region. The distillers must schedule the delivery of the grains from the farms to coincide with the milling and distilling process. At the distillery, the grains are milled to a specific grind size determined by the distiller to make them easier to cook or mash. The milled grains are mixed with water and yeast, a process known as mashing. The distiller then heats the mash to a specific temperature in large cooking tanks while stirring, to release the sugars in the starch.

**FERMENTATION**. Yeast transforms sugar into alcohol during the fermenting process, which happens in massive open-air and closed vats. Yeast strains are very important in this process, and each distillery has its own signature strain that they use to yield the flavors they want in the final product. The yeasts will produce a simple, natural alcohol called ethanol or ethyl alcohol. At this point, sour mash, the leftover mash from a previous distillation, can be added to the mixture; this reduces the mash's pH level to prevent bacteria growth. Once fermentation is complete, distillers strain off the liquid, which is now ready for distillation.

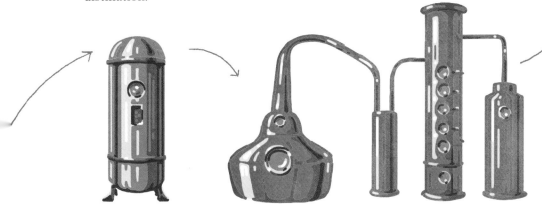

The fermented mash is then distilled.

**DISTILLATION**. Distilling is a process that purifies a liquid by heating and vaporizing it, then collecting the vapor as it condenses into a liquid. The resulting liquid is called a distillate. Distillers will use either a pot still or a column still—both made out of copper or stainless steel—to process the liquid.

During this process, many of the liquid's inherent impurities are left behind, leaving a pure, clean distillate. Many bourbons are distilled twice or more to further purify the base alcohol.

**BARRELS AND AGING.** Once the bourbon reaches between 80 and 125 proof, distillers must transfer the alcohol into a new oak barrel that has been charred. Charred oak barrels are unique to the bourbon industry, and they come from a place called a cooperage that shapes and toasts the barrels. The barrels are filled with the distillate and plugged and placed in a building called a rickhouse to rest. Distillers must now decide how long to age their bourbon before they bottle and sell it. There is a lot of variation in this step of the process: The liquid must age for at least two years before it can legally be called straight bourbon. The bourbon can be aged for the legal minimum amount of time, or it can be aged longer—up to twenty years and beyond. Each year is called a cycle. In the winter, the barrels contract, absorbing the liquid into the oak staves; during the summer, the wood expands, releasing the liquid. Each cycle of contraction and expansion adds more depth, color, and flavor to the bourbon. Furthermore, each year the bourbon spends in the barrel, a natural evaporation process occurs, and that lost liquid is called the "angel's share." The more the bourbon evaporates, the more intense the flavors in the barrel become, but that also means more of the product is being lost, which results in a smaller yield.

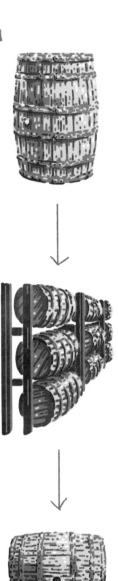

The distillate is transferred to barrels that age in a rickhouse until ready to dump.

**BLENDING AND BOTTLING.** Once the bourbon is mature enough, the barrels are emptied, or "dumped," into large blending tanks and the bourbon is put through a number of rigorous taste tests. At this point, the master distiller or taster will approve the final product, making sure the bourbon is consistent with the flavor of what was released in previous bottlings of the same label. Many bourbons are diluted or cut with water to achieve the final proof level that each distillery determines based on the product they are bottling. Some bourbon is bottled at barrel proof, which means no water has been added. This usually results in a much higher-proof bourbon. The final step is the bottling process, in which the liquid is poured into proprietary bottles. The bottles are sealed, labeled, inspected, and shipped out to your favorite bar, restaurant, liquor store, or gift shop for public consumption.

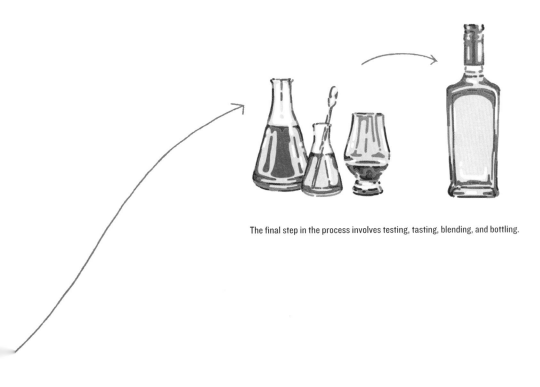

The final step in the process involves testing, tasting, blending, and bottling.

# A BRIEF HISTORY
# OF BOURBON

This brief history serves to revisit the rich and oftentimes shadowy history of a spirit whose origins will never be precisely documented. "History" is a dubious word to use when writing about the origins of bourbon, as so much of it is uncatalogued, unwritten, intentionally obfuscated, or just plain myth. But if you're looking for a more detailed history of bourbon, I can point you to several people from whom I have learned so much and whose impeccable research informs these pages: Fred Minnick, Clay Risen, Susan Reigler, Chuck Cowdery, Reid Mitenbuler, Michael Veach, Eric Zandona, and Ashlie Danielle Stevens (see Further Reading, page 281).

Alcohol, in the form of wine, beer, and spirits, was as important to the early settlers as anything else they brought with them from Europe. Stills from Scotland were used to make an early, and probably rough-tasting, whiskey from leftover crops like potatoes, grains, berries, and apples. As settlers moved westward in the early eighteenth century, decades before Kentucky would become a state, Scots-Irish and German farmers found land west of Pennsylvania and Virginia by traveling on boats along the Ohio River or through the Cumberland Gap and down the Wilderness Road. Regardless of which route they took, they had to cross the unforgiving terrain of the Appalachian Mountains. This is an important piece of history to remember, as these early settlers were, by and large, tough, stubborn, and independent people who risked death to start a new life in the uncharted territories beyond Appalachia. They liked their freedom, and they liked their whiskey even more.

Early stills in Kentucky were made from wood and scrap metal, and it is generally acknowledged that the whiskey coming off these backyard mechanisms was barely potable swill used for the sole purpose of getting drunk. A couple of things happened that led to the birth of what we now call bourbon. First, corn

Men fill and weigh bourbon casks at Labrot and Graham Distillery, now known as Woodford Reserve.

was plentiful in the region. When settlers had the opportunity to rename a small island in the Ohio River off the coast of Louisville, they chose the name Corn Island. Back then, whiskey was made with excess crops after harvest. With corn being so readily available, it became a popular ingredient for making whiskey. And because of the grain's high starch content, the resulting liquor had a sweet taste to it. Additionally, Kentucky ran rich with mineral-packed limestone water, which promoted fermentation and aided in filtering out foul-tasting impurities in the distillate.

The second thing that happened was the Whiskey Rebellion. In 1791, George Washington introduced an excise tax on liquor. This was a way for Congress to climb out of the national debt, and they defended this new tax by explaining it as a sin tax or luxury tax (which is shockingly still the reasoning used today for taxing alcoholic beverages at a higher rate than other beverages). This infuriated the nation's distillers, who were also farmers, and who were not by any means rich. Without getting into the complex details of the Whiskey Rebellion, it is enough to say that revolts led to uprisings, which led to violence, mostly in the states of Pennsylvania and Maryland, where there was already an established whiskey industry, albeit mostly rye whiskey. By this time, Kentucky was a commonwealth, and many distillers moved to

Kentucky to escape the harsh consequences of their unsuccessful rebellion. They brought with them a knowledge of whiskey making, and in Kentucky, they discovered this sweet new frontier liquor being made from corn. Enter the age of bourbon.

So when did this New World whiskey officially transition into "bourbon"? Traditional lore highlights the "godfathers of American bourbon" like Elijah Craig, who is said to have been the first to age the product in charred oak casks (a requisite for making bourbon), and Jacob Spears, who was allegedly the first to label his product "Bourbon whiskey." There is also the story of Evan

Williams, who built the first commercial distillery. Typical of the time, the labor of enslaved Black farmworkers, who most certainly played an integral role in the production of whiskey, is largely missing from these accounts.

An even bigger mystery is how bourbon came to be called bourbon. According to John T. Edge's *The New Encyclopedia of Southern Culture: Foodways*, bourbon may have been called such after Virginia's Bourbon County, which was established in 1785. This was a huge county that encompassed parts of Eastern Kentucky. When Kentucky separated from Virginia and became a new state in 1792, its legislators created their own Bourbon County.

Employees load bourbon bottles onto a conveyor platform at Fitzgerald Distillery in 1912.

Michael Veach, a bourbon historian and author of *Kentucky Bourbon Whiskey: An American Heritage*, posits that the spirit was actually named after Bourbon Street in New Orleans, originally named Rue Bourbon by French engineer Adrien de Pauger in 1712 as a nod to the House of Bourbon, one of Europe's royal dynasties. The street connected to a major port, where shipments of this "new" corn whiskey sold well as an alternative to more expensive French spirits.

Regardless of where the name came from, by the late nineteenth century, many of the elements that make up modern bourbon, like proof and age requirements, were cemented by the Bottled-in-Bond Act of 1897. Bourbon's popularity continued to boom until 1919, when Prohibition absolutely obliterated the industry.

Before Prohibition, historians estimate there were more than five hundred distilleries in Kentucky; when the 18th Amendment was finally repealed in 1933, there were only six. The Kentucky bourbon industry quickly began to rebuild itself, however. By 1938, the number of distilleries had increased to about seventy.

Since then, the industry has been in a continual cycle of booms—such as during the *Mad Men* era of the late 1950s and '60s—and busts. As Chuck Cowdery noted in his 2004 book *Bourbon, Straight*, consumption of bourbon fell in favor of clear spirits every year from 1978 until the mid-2000s. But then the modern bourbon boom began to take flight. According to the Kentucky Distillers' Association, the total value of Kentucky's inventoried bourbon stock surged from $800 million in 2006 to over $1 billion in 2007, and the bourbon boom shows no clear signs that a substantial bust is on the horizon. In 2022, the Kentucky Distillers' Association estimated that Kentucky bourbon is now a $9 billion dollar industry.

There are a number of theories as to why. There was the advent of the craft cocktail renaissance, which had bartenders (and patrons) reaching for brown liquor to make classics like the old-fashioned and the Manhattan. Around that time, the price of Scotch had also gone sky-high, so many consumers reached for bourbon as a then-cheaper alternative. There is also the theory that after the tragic events in NYC on 9/11, there was a rallying cry of patriotism that rippled through everything from food to art to alcohol. And what is more American than bourbon? Shortly thereafter, there was also the phenomenon known as Anthony Bourdain, a wildly influential figure in the world of food and drink culture. When he began to gush about bourbon and his love for Pappy Van Winkle, there was an immediate ripple effect throughout the restaurant and bar industry, leading to higher demand for this newfound Kentucky bourbon. Clay Risen, in his seminal book *Bourbon*, suggests that the renaissance was really just a return to the whiskey-drinking culture that had been part of America's identity from the frontier era to the 1950s and '60s. Whatever the reason, I'm happier because of it.

# HOW TO COOK WITH BOURBON

There isn't any secret technique to cooking with bourbon. It can be as simple as throwing in a splash here and there to flavor a dish as you see fit. Or it can be a more calculated and nuanced effort. There are a number of things to remember about bourbon that will help you out in your own bourbon cooking journey.

## Bourbon Is Not Wine

Bourbon is high proof, meaning it's got a lot of alcohol in it. It is not wine, and you cannot substitute the same amount of wine for bourbon in a recipe. Wine is made from grapes, so it has a very fruity quality, whereas bourbon is much stronger and has a multitude of flavors, the most dominant being caramel, char, leather, and hay. Many of the recipes featured here will instruct you to reduce the bourbon before it goes into a recipe. There are two reasons for that. First, it intensifies the flavor of the bourbon. Second, it burns off the alcohol (or ethanol), which boils and evaporates at a much lower temperature than water. So when you boil bourbon in a pot, the ethanol will evaporate first, leaving behind a relatively alcohol-free liquid with concentrated bourbon flavor. This is the juice we are generally looking for when cooking with bourbon. But a few careful reminders about this process:

- The easiest way to tell if the ethanol has cooked out of your bourbon is to waft a bit of the steam from the pot toward your nose and breathe in. Heated ethanol will burn the inside of your nose and cause a coughing reaction. If all you can smell is bourbon aroma and your nostrils aren't burning, your bourbon is ready.

- Even if you boil bourbon for extended periods of time, the liquid is never 100 percent alcohol-free, so if you are cooking for someone who cannot drink alcohol, do not allow them to taste the reduced bourbon thinking it is a nonalcoholic product.

- Ethanol is volatile and will ignite very easily when heated. Which means you could easily end up with a pot of flaming bourbon raging in your kitchen. Be very careful when you cook with any distilled spirit. Do not hold your face over the pot looking into the liquid. I have done this before and found myself without eyelashes for weeks.

- If and when your bourbon ignites, stay calm. The best way to tamp out the flame is to turn off your heat source and then quickly put a tight-fitting lid over the pot. Always have a lid at the ready to put out a potential fire before you start cooking with bourbon. Once you put the pot back on the heat, the bourbon will almost always reignite. I've found that covering the pot partially with its lid and cooking over medium heat is the best way to boil off the ethanol with minimal flames.

- You want to boil off the ethanol in dishes that will be served warm because the smell and taste of warm ethanol is not a pleasant culinary experience. In many cold and room-temperature dishes and desserts, however, it is actually pleasant to have the bite of alcohol lingering in your mouth, so you'll notice a number of recipes do not require you to burn off the alcohol. If you do not like the sensation of alcohol in your food, by all means, reduce and boil off the ethanol in any recipe that doesn't explicitly require it.

## Bourbon's Flavors

Five core elements make up the identity of bourbon: fire, corn, oak, yeast, and copper. Within these five components are the keys to bourbon's flavors. (Water is the sixth element, but it is not a component of flavor.) One could argue that the most important element to bourbon is time, but that is more of a philosophical idea.

To make an overall generalization, bourbon draws toasted or smoky notes from the charred barrels, sweet and vegetal notes from the corn, spice and vanilla notes from the oak that makes up the barrels, umami and floral notes from the yeast, and, finally, a clean and consistent flavor from the copper in the still. Copper is a miracle element that makes the distillation process safe and consistent. It conducts heat evenly and quickly, which is why in the pastry world, sugars are cooked in copper, giving us the warm gift of caramel—a flavor so rooted in bourbon that it is often the first thing that comes to people's minds when they are asked what bourbon tastes like.

I'm not a huge proponent of obscure tasting notes (you know, when people sip wine and say they can taste grass and asphalt and lemon verbena), but they are helpful as notions to push your palate in specific directions. I don't believe in right or wrong descriptors, and the ones I use in this book are merely suggestions. But what fascinates me about bourbon is that it has many flavors that pull in different directions. I don't know if I have ever tasted wood-fired rutabaga in a glass of bourbon, but I can recognize flavors that I divide into two categories: sweet and savory.

The sweet flavors are up front, at the tip of the tongue, and they're the most obvious: caramel, butterscotch, orange, toffee, raisiny notes, and, without getting too pretentious, I would even go as far as to say a warm cinnamon apple pie flavor.

The savory notes register in the back of your mouth; they come to you after the sweet notes dissipate: lightly burnt toast, dried hay, coffee, spices like nutmeg and black pepper, aged leather (and yes, I have put old leather in my mouth to see if the comparison is accurate—it is). What's remarkable about bourbon is that all these seemingly diverse flavors can coexist at the same time in one glass. So when I think about how to use bourbon as an ingredient, I isolate one or more of these flavor notes and manipulate the rest of the ingredients in the dish to bring them out. For example, if I want to highlight the butterscotch in the bourbon, I will add butterscotch to the dish, and that will make me taste the bourbon through the lens of butterscotch, which makes the savory notes fade. They're still there, but in the distance, adding complexity to the dish while I still get the punch of butterscotch up front. This is my general approach to cooking with bourbon, and you'll see this at work in the recipes in this book.

# Bourbons for Cooking

This is subjective, and don't let anyone tell you what you can or cannot do with your bourbon. We all have our favorites, and once you've paid good money to purchase your bourbon, you can do whatever you want with it. Having said that, here are a few rules that will act as guardrails to keep you on a productive path.

- Don't waste your money cooking with an expensive bourbon (usually aged bourbon that has layers of complex notes). Any time you cook with alcohol, be it wine, cognac, or bourbon, the heat will destroy a lot of those delicate nuances, which is what you're paying top dollar for. Also, many bourbons are expensive because they are rare, not necessarily because they're better quality. So don't always equate price with quality.

- The brand of bourbon you select doesn't matter. The more important designation is the mash bill. Generally there are two kinds of bourbon: **WHEATED BOURBONS** use predominantly wheat as the secondary ingredient in the mash bill after corn. This will result in a sweeter, softer bourbon. These bourbons are generally good for use in desserts. The other bourbon (for our purpose) is what I will call a **SPICED BOURBON**. These bourbons use a combination of rye, barley, or malts as their secondary grain in the mash bill after corn. This will result in a spicier finish with more bitter notes. This is the bourbon I generally use for savory dishes. There is a trend right now to bottle double oaked or extra oak bourbon. I find that these bourbons, though great for drinking, are too aggressive for cooking, especially when you reduce the bourbon and concentrate its flavor even further.

- In terms of age statements, my general rule of thumb is never to cook with a bourbon that is aged longer than eight years. While it's a treat to cook with a ten-year-old bourbon every once in a while, and a luxury to do so, generally speaking, it's a big ol' waste of money. Most recipes call for reducing bourbon, and when you do, you lose the angelic nuances that make a ten- or twelve-year-old bourbon so precious. Save the older stuff for sipping. Cook with a good five-year-old bourbon and the recipe will turn out just fine.

- Don't worry too much about the brand of bourbon you cook with. As I've said, the mash bill and age statement are more important. But a lot of mash bills are secret, so you don't know the exact recipe in a bourbon. And age statements can be confusing because not all bourbons put their age statements on their labels. When in doubt, pick a bourbon that you like to drink, and it will work just as well in cooking.

Keep in mind that there is no such thing as the best bourbon; you don't even have to have a favorite bourbon. I get asked what my favorite bourbon is all the time, and my answer is always: the one I have in my hand. That's because in order to be called bourbon, all bourbon has to abide by strict rules, so whichever bottle you have will always have quality liquid inside. I pick my bourbons based on their flavor profiles, but sometimes I pick them because I like their story or what the company stands for or because my friend happens to work at the distillery. There are no bad choices. I do always cheer for Kentucky bourbons, mainly because the people in the commonwealth have been making them the longest. Nothing can account for the history and the know-how that have been passed down for generations in Kentucky. I laud Kentucky bourbon because I have roots here in Kentucky, because the story of bourbon is part of the fabric of my life. The rest of the country is playing catch-up in the bourbon game, in my opinion. But if you like and want to cook with a bourbon from your home state, by all means, go for it.

# FIRE AND TOAST

"Always carry a flagon of
whiskey in case of snakebite
and, furthermore, always
carry a small snake."

—W. C. FIELDS

There is no bourbon without fire. No other whiskey in the world requires that
the barrels that hold the whiskey be charred before aging. The control of fire
is proof of human intelligence. Fire is mesmerizing and destructive. We are
attracted to it and scared of it. Fire is the origin of cooking. The flavor that
fire imparts to food is foundational. I have always been seduced by the flavor
imparted by an open flame. It goes by many names: charred, grilled, burnt,
toasted, smoked. It is the Maillard reaction; it is ashes and bark; it is barbecue
and grilling. The craving is instinctual.

Food that is charred or grilled has an obvious pairing advantage with bourbon. As a chef, knowing more about the relationship between fire and bourbon
helps me understand how to cook with it, what to pair with it, and how the relationship between food and bourbon works. Bourbon doesn't use many ingredients: water, corn, grains, yeast. But distilling and aging are processes that have
evolved over time and that contribute to the bourbon's flavor: wood for barrels,
copper for distillation, time. Fire is what makes bourbon unique; it is the identity of bourbon at its core.

The addition of fire to the bourbon-making process happens at a place called
a cooperage, where barrels are built and then charred. It's not a place most people get to visit. (Any place where you have temperatures up to 1500°F is a place
that requires extreme caution.) Cooperages do not offer tours; they don't have
gift shops. But of all the places related to bourbon—the distillery, the rickhouse,
the grain fields—the cooperage is the place I love to visit the most.

At the Independent Stave Company cooperage in Morehead, Kentucky, they make barrels for many of the bourbons you're likely familiar with. You can smell the burning wood from the parking lot: It's the smoky campfire smell of burning oak staves. It's so familiar and comforting, it immediately warms me through to my bones. When you walk onto the floor of a cooperage, the smell is a hundred times more intense. It is vanilla and smoke and toasted almond. It is so loud, it's difficult to hear what the person standing next to you is saying. Pistons release steam in regular intervals. Barrel rings hit the concrete floor and the sound echoes throughout the factory. Galvanized iron rings are hammered onto barrels, creating a drum sound that vibrates through their empty bellies. Waves of heat pulse through the air and bake your cheeks. Embers crash in waves and float in front of you like fairies. The heat comes from blasting fire guns. It is controlled and wild. It is violent and hypnotic. I could stand there for hours watching the barrels burn.

Hollow barrels arrive on conveyor belts before their heads have been attached. It takes only seconds to burn the inside of a barrel with a jet of flame. Each distiller has a different char amount they want for their bourbon. Much of this is secretive. When the blasting gun is finished, the sizzling barrels are rolled into a warehouse for storage before being assembled and shipped off. When you enter this part of the cooperage, you can smell bourbon, even though you know there isn't a drop of alcohol in this factory. Just the smell of newly burnt oak barrels is enough to trigger your brain to believe you're standing inside a library of old whiskey bottles. It is vanilla and caramel, smoke and spices. All these flavors, previously dormant in the white oak staves, have been liberated and now await the distillate that will absorb them.

Outside the cooperage are stacks of wood as far as the eye can see, an entire city of oak staves air-drying in the Kentucky sun. These staves come in from the sawmills as stiff oak boards, dormant and moist. They get air-seasoned anywhere from three to twelve months, then kiln-dried for about thirty days. They get arranged into a cylinder shape and then steamed at 160°F to bend them into the classic bellied barrel shape. Six metal hoops hold the barrel together. Roughly the same process happens at every cooperage, but there are slight differences in technique at each one.

A little over an hour away from Independent Stave is Kelvin Cooperage in Louisville. It sits on a small plot of land next to an auto junkyard. It's what you might call a craft cooperage, though they still produce about 350 barrels a day. Paul McLaughlin's office is a small, nondescript white-walled cubicle with a wooden table crowded with some of my favorite bourbons. Paul is from Scotland. His father quit school at age fifteen to apprentice at a cooperage in Glasgow. Paul's brother did the same when he was sixteen. Paul joined the family business soon thereafter. They then started a cooperage business with his brother, Kevin, on the banks of the River Kelvin in Glasgow. Scotch and bourbon have a symbiotic bond, as many Scotch producers age their whiskey in spent bourbon barrels. That's how Paul found his way to Kentucky from Scotland. Originally, the brothers were buying used barrels and repairing them for the Scotch industry. After a while, it made more sense to operate in Kentucky and repair the barrels there before shipping them to Scotland. Paul and Kevin set up Kelvin Cooperage in Louisville. At first, they dealt only in used bourbon barrels. But when the bourbon craft boom happened, they started making their own barrels, and they haven't stopped a day since.

The fire Paul produces for charring barrels comes from oak burned in a firepot; he uses no gas. When he makes the round barrel heads, he cuts a circle out of a square piece of wood. The excess wood cut from the corners is all he uses to fuel his firepots. Unlike most cooperages, Paul also toasts the wood before charring it. His first experience making barrels was for the wine industry, where barrels are toasted but not charred. He transferred that expertise to whiskey barrels. Toasting before charring takes longer and it slows down the barrel production pace, but he believes it adds to the flavor of the bourbon that gets aged in his barrels. "When we slowly toast the wood, we get almondy, marzipan notes as the wood sugars activate and generate furfural [a strong-scented aldehyde]," says Paul. "Then we char the oak, but the toast layer is still underneath, so over time, the bourbon is getting interaction with both layers. It gives the bourbon a pronounced middle palate that you don't get with simply charred wood."

When you run your fingers along the inside of a charred barrel, the burnt oak staves leave a thick layer of residue on your skin—sticky, resin filled, almost creamy. It is not ash, which is dead and flaky. It is oily and tarlike. It doesn't wash off easily. This is what the clear corn liquor that comes off the still will interact with, quietly, in a rickhouse, over many summers and winters, over the course of years. Kentucky has hot summers and cold winters. When it's cold, the wood constricts and absorbs the liquid. When the temperature rises, the wood expands and releases the liquid. This is called a cycle or a season. Each time this happens, the liquid reacts with the wood and the char, getting darker with each season, getting richer, and slowly metamorphosing from corn liquor to bourbon. Each time this happens, a little bit of the bourbon evaporates, the angel's share, and the liquid concentrates.

So what does this do for flavor? It adds smokiness and toasted notes. It intensifies the vanillin in the oak. Fire and time mellow the corn flavor. The char on the oak acts as a carbon filter, taking away many of the rough notes of the corn distillate that entered the barrel. The resulting bourbon isn't burnt; something happens in the process where the oak, the fire, the corn, and the water stop tasting like individual elements and merge into one golden elixir that possesses all of these qualities. It is only then that we call it a bourbon.

# THE COOPER

# PAUL McLAUGHLIN

Cooperages are the unsung heroes of bourbon. They are where oak staves are aged, steamed, toasted, charred, and shaped into bourbon barrels. The iconic bourbon barrel is an image we see emblazoned on every piece of bourbon marketing, but visitors rarely get to see the inside of a cooperage. Paul McLaughlin has been tied to the cooperage business since his childhood in Scotland, where his father founded Kelvin Cooperage. Though he swore he would never enter his father's business, Paul, with his late brother, Kevin, joined the cooperage in 2001 and eventually moved their operation to Kentucky. Together, they turned it into one of the most reputable whiskey barrel manufacturers for the craft distilling industry.

**Q:** *When do you drink Scotch and when do you drink bourbon?*

**A:** Typically, whenever they are offered! Seriously, my favorite times to drink either spirit are when a friend or a customer has something in particular that they want to share with me because something about it has spoken to them.

**Q:** *What does fire or toasting add to the flavor of bourbon?*

**A:** When we toast the barrels, we are activating all the desirable American oak flavor profiles that people have grown to love. We look for a very particular smell. Lots of people describe it as campfire or toasted marshmallows. I look for a marzipan, almondy smell that tells me we have hit the sweet spot. The toast layer is an additive layer of flavor, while the char layer acts as a carbon filter. It is the interplay of these two layers that forms the basis of the magic that the barrel adds to the spirit.

**Q:** *How did you get started in the cooperage business?*

**A:** My father started Kelvin Cooperage in 1963 in Scotland. My brother followed him into the business, and I happily vowed that I would never join the family business. It took only a few years of practicing law for me to realize that perhaps the cooperage industry wasn't so bad after all. Twenty-plus years later, I am still here.

**Q:** *Which do you prefer: the cuisine of Scotland or the cuisine of Kentucky?*

**A:** Like a lot of people, I miss certain foods from growing up in Scotland—Irn-Bru, black pudding, and haggis, to name a few. I am fortunate to travel back to Scotland enough to satisfy those cravings. Along with its thriving bourbon scene, Louisville has great restaurants, so I feel like I'm doing pretty well here. Although I must confess that I haven't acquired a taste for Hot Brown yet.

**Q:** *Do you think bourbon will catch on in Europe and other countries outside the United States?*

**A:** I think we're already seeing it happen. I always pay attention to what is available in bars and liquor stores in Europe, and bourbon is definitely increasing its footprint. It used to be the same few brands that were widely available in Europe, but it seems like the variety of brands available is growing and the selection is improving. We are making a lot of bourbon in the United States, so we will need these export markets to continue to grow with bourbon.

# A HISTORY OF
# KENTUCKY COOPERAGES

One of the earliest depictions of coopers—craftsmen who are trained to make wooden vessels using timber staves and metal or wooden binding rings—was found in a wall painting in the tomb of Hesy-Ra, an Egyptian high official. Historians date the painting to about 2600 BCE.

In the thousands of years since then, coopers have been integral to everyday life. Pliny the Elder, the Roman historian, wrote that the Gauls would store beverages in wooden casks made by coopers; in ancient Greece, casks were similarly used to store alcohol (though Julius Caesar was known for filling them with tar and catapulting them as a wartime weapon). In the Middle Ages, coopers worked with winemakers and brewers to store mead and ale, much like modern-day coopers are employed by distilleries to ensure their bourbon is aged properly.

It's a specialized job, and that has been the case since the early days of colonial America, when it took seven years for an apprentice to become a cooper. Coopering is also deeply important to bourbon's quality. The barrel contributes over 50 percent of the bourbon's flavor and 100 percent of its color.

To make bourbon barrels, coopers place slabs of wood by hand into a machine that shapes each slab (known as a stave) to a very specific angle so they'll fit together to form the barrel's convex sides. Those staves are placed in a metal ring, then wrapped with additional rings to solidify the barrel shape. The barrels are heated for pliability and then charred for flavor. The toasting starts a caramelization process, which eventually imbues the bourbon with flavors such as caramel, vanilla, tobacco, and smoke. Once cooled, the barrel is cauterized and sealed, and a hole is drilled into the side. After checking for leaks (using water, not spirits), the coopers send them out to their eventual homes.

No definitive historical text explains why bourbon barrels had to be charred, but there seems to be a general consensus that barrels in Kentucky were used

for more than just whiskey. Everything was shipped in barrels—fish, oil, cured meats, etc. When it came time to ship whiskey in barrels to be floated downriver, most likely to New Orleans, the inside of the barrels was charred to get rid of any leftover flavors and smells. Customers who drank whiskey from these charred barrels noticed it had a pleasant quality to it, and over time, this led to the tradition of charring new barrels.

Another likely story is that during the process of toasting wood staves for bending, some of the staves may have accidentally been charred. Nowadays, most cooperages will steam the staves to make them pliable, but back then, they were heated over open fires. Oak is a very hard wood, and it takes exposure to a lot of heat over a long period of time to bend oak staves. As the story goes, a less-than-attentive worker burned a batch of oak staves by accident, and those staves ended up in a barrel that was later recognized as lending the bourbon inside a more pronounced and pleasant flavor.

The craft of a cooperage is often passed from generation to generation, and it is intrinsically tied to Kentucky's lumber industry. American white oak is Kentucky's most commercially important timber oak, in large part because of its use in whiskey barrel production, generating millions of dollars in revenue for the commonwealth each year.

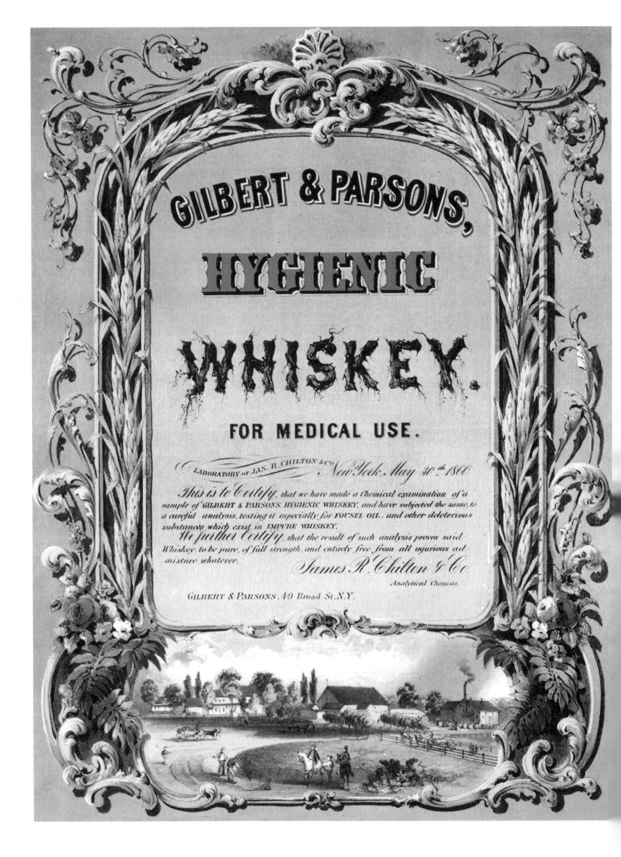

# BOURBON DURING PROHIBITION

"Civilization started with distillation."
—WILLIAM FAULKNER

While the nascent bourbon industry was picking up steam in the mid-1800s, so was another movement made up of mostly women who were sick and tired of their husbands, fathers, and brothers wasting their nights away in saloons. This was dubbed the temperance movement. It was composed of various organizations, including the Protestant Church, the Women's Christian Temperance Union (endorsed by Susan B. Anthony), and the Anti-Saloon League. This nationwide movement eventually led to the passage of the Volstead Act of 1919, also known as the National Prohibition Act, which made the production, sale, and transport of "intoxicating" liquors illegal. This act destroyed most of the whiskey industry, both nationally and in Kentucky, though a few distilleries were granted permission to bottle bourbon for medicinal purposes. Those distilleries were American Medicinal Spirits, Schenley Distilling Company, James Thompson & Brother, Frankfort Distilling Company, Brown-Forman, and A. Ph. Stitzel Distillery. There were also "medicinal" and "hygienic" concoctions being sold like the one advertised by Gilbert & Parsons that promised health under the guise of legal whiskey.

Though Prohibition devastated the bourbon industry, most historians agree that during this time, the general public were not leading lives of abstinence. The thirteen years of Prohibition gave rise to a wave of illegal practices, mass corruption, and

Some whiskey bottles were labeled for medicinal use during Prohibition.

Monitored by police
and federal officers,
men pour alcohol
into the sewer
during Prohibition.

a level of organized crime that the United States had never known before. If you were an affluent Kentuckian, for example, you could still purchase whiskey, as long as it was prescribed by a doctor. The packaging had to be stamped with a government seal, and it had to be sold at 100 proof, but a suffering patient with a doctor willing to fill out a prescription could receive up to one pint of bourbon every ten days.

Running parallel to this legal form of sale were, of course, moonshining and bootlegging. The making of whiskey and grain spirits went underground as small illegal stills popped up all throughout the South, hidden in backyard cabins and wooded areas. This whiskey was then transported by organized crime units to various speakeasies in Chicago, New York City, and other metropolitan areas. This element of Prohibition tends to be the most romanticized, largely because it dovetails with so many interesting characters.

George Remus was a defense attorney from Chicago who exploited the Prohibition prescription system to make liquor available to the masses. A former pharmacist who owned both distilleries and pharmaceutical companies, he created a scheme whereby he pulled permits to withdraw whiskey, then had that whiskey stolen by his own people and distributed to various outlets while he reported it as stolen. His wealth and fame became so well known that F. Scott Fitzgerald's *The Great Gatsby* is rumored to be loosely based on his life.

The Prohibition period has been heavily glamorized in books and movies, but it was one of the most corrupt and bloody eras in modern American history. It gave rise to a generation of gangsters, mobsters, and money launderers who have become Hollywood legends. Names like Lucky Luciano, Dutch Schultz, Meyer Lansky, Bugsy Siegel, and the legendary Al Capone are synonymous with Prohibition. The endless movies and books about them are proof that their influence over the whiskey business and America has had lasting effects that can still be felt today. For example, the three-tier distribution system of alcohol that currently exists today is modeled after the distribution system that organized crime invented during Prohibition.

On December 5, 1933, Prohibition was finally repealed. Bourbon distillers and businesspeople were left to pick up the pieces and remake an industry that had been demolished and corrupted.

# LAPSANG SOUCHONG MANHATTAN

Beverage manager Stacie Stewart has worked closely with me for years, developing cocktails for two different restaurants of mine. Her take on a smoky Manhattan is indicative of her globally minded approach to cocktails and her love for deep, haunting flavors.

**Makes 1**

¼ cup loose Lapsang souchong tea

10 ounces bourbon

½ ounce oloroso sherry

⅛ teaspoon pure vanilla extract

1 barrel-aged cherry, for garnish

Measure the tea into a large container with a tight-fitting lid. Add the bourbon. Cover tightly, swirl the container rapidly, and let rest for 10 minutes. This limited contact between the tea and the bourbon will impart the smokiness of the tea but only a small amount of the tannins.

When 10 minutes have elapsed, set a fine-mesh strainer over a large measuring cup and pour the washed bourbon through it. Store the bourbon in a decanter or bottle.

In a mixing glass, combine 2 ounces of the tea-washed bourbon, the sherry, and the vanilla. Add a fair amount of ice to the glass and stir for 15 to 20 seconds; this drink really opens up with some dilution. Strain the cocktail into your favorite glass and garnish with a barrel-aged cherry.

> "The great thing about bourbon now, in the age of transparency, is that the artistry of the makers can really be appreciated fully. We're seeing really talented people *crafting* a product, making it theirs."
>
> **—STACIE STEWART**

# WHAT GLASS SHOULD I USE TO DRINK BOURBON?

A big part of our sense of taste is actually dependent on how well we are able to smell the food or drink in front of us. That's why a collective of master blenders from five of the largest whiskey companies in Scotland put their heads together with Glencairn Crystal in 2001 to create the perfect glass for tasting, and smelling, whiskey.

The Glencairn glass has a rounded bottom and a tapered center and top, almost like an early-season tulip, and was the first style of glass to receive an official endorsement from the Scotch Whisky Association. Its design is optimal for trapping aromas in the glass, enabling drinkers to take their time tasting and testing the drink. When you visit distillery sampling rooms around Kentucky, you'll likely see miniature versions of the Glencairn glass.

If you're drinking a cocktail or sipping in the comfort of your own home, the answer to what glass you should use is any glass that you have on hand. There is no wrong vessel for drinking bourbon. I'm partial to an oversize rocks glass with a few ice cubes and a shallow finger of bourbon. But I've also enjoyed it equally as much in a plastic cup with chipped ice.

The shape of the Glencairn glass captures the aroma at the base of the glass and directs it up the narrow neck with a small flare at the rim that diffuses the perfume up to your nose. It is a perfect shape for swirling and sipping.

# ICE CUBES AND WHISKEY

Let's face it: For most of us, ice is just something that chills the liquid in our glass. Most of the time, I couldn't care less about the ice in my bourbon, and nothing irritates me more than a thirty-minute discussion about the purity of ice. I'm not going to tell you which ice pairs well with which cocktails. But ice *is* an essential component in most bourbon drinks, so it's helpful to know what all the fascination is about.

- **CUBES:** Ice cubes—the kind found in home freezers and many bar wells—have their benefits with bourbon. These can take the form of small cubes, crescent shapes, or nuggets, but all serve the same purpose. Cubes are small, so they freeze quickly and chill drinks quickly. But smaller ice shapes melt quickly as well, meaning they can overdilute one's whiskey.

- **BLOCKS AND SPHERES:** Block cubes and ice spheres are made using large rubber molds or intricate ice makers that produce large squares or jumbo balls of ice. These take longer to freeze, but they have the benefit of melting much, much slower. And they look cool in your oversize rocks glass.

- **STONES**: Whiskey stones, or whiskey rocks, are small cubes of clean natural stone (typically soapstone) that can be frozen and used to chill whiskey and other spirits. Increasingly, versions made of polished metal are also available. The big advantage, of course, is that they won't melt and dilute the bourbon. However, some critics claim that the mineral content—or the metal content—of the stones can impact the natural flavor of the bourbon. And if you like to chew on your ice like I do, it's easy to forget that the cold nugget between your teeth is a stone, resulting in an unexpected visit to the dentist.

- **CRUSHED**: If you've ever had a mint julep or a bourbon slushie, it was likely served with crushed, flaked, or pellet ice. If you're not willing to spend the money on a dedicated ice maker, then do what most bartenders do and use a Lewis bag, a small, sturdy canvas bag made for crushing ice. Put standard ice cubes in the bag and go to town on them with a wooden mallet, a meat tenderizer, or a heavy pan. (At home, you can use two dish towels instead of a Lewis bag for a similar effect.)

Ice clarity is also a sought-after trait for ice cube connoisseurs. Complete translucence can be achieved by boiling water, sometimes multiple times, and then slow-freezing it into cubes, which are then stored in airtight containers to preserve their look and prevent freezer burn. Making such pristine ice is labor-intensive, but the look on your guests' faces when they see a crystal-clear cube is priceless.

# FIRE IS ESSENTIAL, BUT SO IS WATER

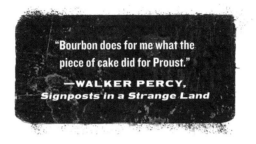

"Bourbon does for me what the piece of cake did for Proust."

—WALKER PERCY, *Signposts in a Strange Land*

Geographically speaking, limestone underlies huge swaths of land in and around Appalachia, including much of Kentucky. The water that percolates through those limestone deposits—often called hard water or limestone water—is special. It has a high pH, which promotes fermentation, and is packed with minerals like calcium and magnesium carbonates. Additionally, it filters out impurities, including iron, which can imbue bourbon with a metallic taste and discolor the final spirit.

Kentucky's limestone geology means that iron and other impurities are naturally filtered out of the water as it flows over the rock, making it mineral-rich and naturally sweet-tasting. Limestone water is enough a part of the lore of Kentucky bourbon that most distillery tours will mention it as the reason bourbon from the commonwealth is so unique. This isn't *un*true, but most distilleries are using some variation of filtered and reverse-osmosis water to make a smooth, consistent product. Some distilleries in Kentucky still use water from natural sources; Maker's Mark has its own water source and watershed on the distillery campus, for example, while Buffalo Trace gets some of its water from the Kentucky River and natural springs in Frankfort. Most distilleries, though, use municipally treated water, which—as Louisville Water Company scientist Mark Campbell has written—still has high levels of calcium and high alkalinity but is stripped of iron.

So, yes, the water does matter even though it may not be sourced from the romantic images of backwoods Kentucky waterways.

# WHAT'S IN A LABEL?

Reading a bourbon label is like deciphering a code written in a foreign language. Some of it is very technical, and some of it is very antiquated. All of it can be a little confusing. Here's a quick primer on how to read a bourbon label.

## ABV and Proof

Bourbon bottles may show the liquor's proof, its ABV, or both.

ABV (alcohol by volume) is a universal metric used to determine what percentage of a beverage's total volume is pure alcohol. When you see this number on a bottle, you can use it to determine the amount of pure alcohol in a serving of bourbon. For instance, a 2-ounce pour of bourbon with 40% ABV contains 0.8 ounce of pure alcohol.

Proof indicates the strength of a liquor based on its ethanol content. On modern American spirits bottles, proof is simply the liquor's ABV multiplied by two, so a 40% ABV bourbon would be referred to as 80 proof. Historically, proof was a less scientific measure of alcohol's potency. In sixteenth-century England, liquor that contained higher amounts of alcohol was taxed at higher rates. To test this, government officials would soak gunpowder in the spirit in question, then attempt to ignite it; if it caught fire, that was "proof" of the liquor's strength.

You might also see the term "barrel proof," a federally regulated designation that means the bourbon in the bottle has the same alcohol content (usually over 100 proof), with up to two degrees' difference in ABV, that it did when it was put into the barrel for aging and it hasn't been diluted with water.

## "Bottled in Bond"

The early days of bourbon, from its beginnings in the early 1800s to the boom years at the end of the century, must have been exciting times. But let's not

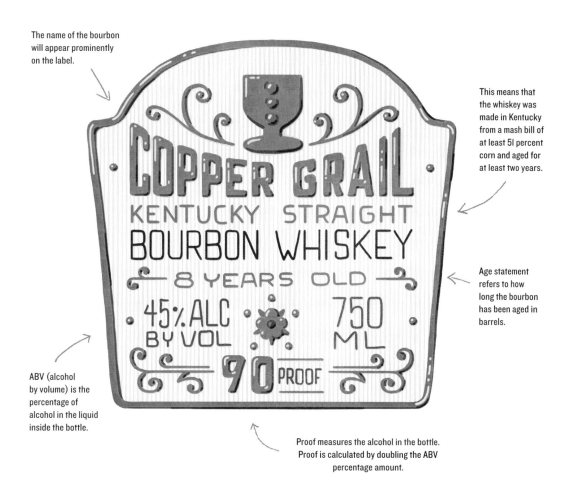

The name of the bourbon will appear prominently on the label.

This means that the whiskey was made in Kentucky from a mash bill of at least 51 percent corn and aged for at least two years.

Age statement refers to how long the bourbon has been aged in barrels.

ABV (alcohol by volume) is the percentage of alcohol in the liquid inside the bottle.

Proof measures the alcohol in the bottle. Proof is calculated by doubling the ABV percentage amount.

COPPER GRAIL
KENTUCKY STRAIGHT
BOURBON WHISKEY
8 YEARS OLD
45% ALC BY VOL
750 ML
90 PROOF

romanticize it too much. There were plenty of grifters, peddlers, and snake oil salesmen attempting to cash in on the rise of bourbon by making an inferior distillate and masking it with caramel color, wood chips, tobacco juice, and glycerin. There was nothing legally to guarantee that what was on the label was actually in the bottle.

The Bottled-in-Bond Act, instituted in 1897, was one of the earliest examples of consumer protection law, and it helped cement what made bourbon a distinctly American spirit. If a bottle bore the bond, which was overseen by the

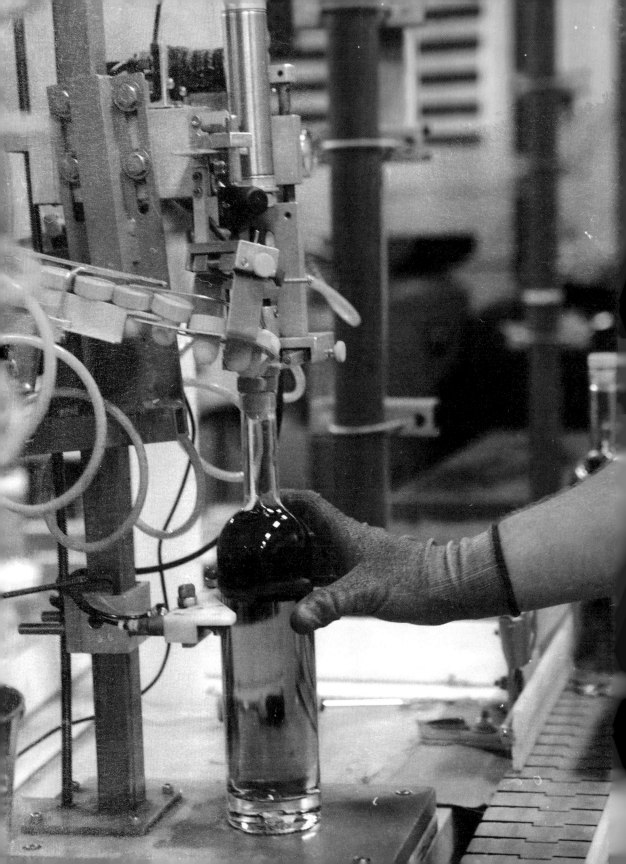

federal government, consumers knew it met certain specifications. The law ensured, among other stipulations, that the spirit was produced in the United States and aged in a federally bonded warehouse for at least four years; that it was bottled at 100 proof; that it was the product of one distillation season by one distiller at one distillery; and that the label on its bottle would identify where it was distilled and bottled.

This was an essential distinction of quality and regulation. But by the 1970s, distillation in America had become legitimate, and the need for a government stamp of approval became less necessary. Also, consumers were acquiring a taste for blended whiskeys that often weren't produced domestically, and bottled-in-bond products lost their luster.

However, bourbon's timeline is a series of busts and booms, and when sales started booming again, alongside the craft cocktail movement in the late 1990s, that bottled-in-bond stamp became coveted again by both distillers and customers.

## Age Statement

An age statement indicates the age of the "youngest" bourbon in a bottle. (Only if a product is single barrel or bottled-in-bond will all the bourbon be the same age.) Any bourbon aged less than four years must include an age statement on its label; after that, an age statement is voluntary, so some bottles have them and others do not. If a bottle doesn't have an age statement, that doesn't mean it's a poor-quality bourbon; it just means it's probably a blended bourbon, which could contain some bourbon from barrels that might be four years old and some from other barrels that could be six or seven years old.

## Distilled Spirits Plant Number

The distilled spirits plant number (or DSP Number/DSPN) is one of the more confusing bits of information on a bourbon bottle, but put simply, it all comes back to the history of how bourbon is taxed.

In preparation for funding the Civil War, President Abraham Lincoln wanted to begin taxing spirits again. There was a debate about how to measure the volume of liquid to be taxed. Bourbon seeps into the barrel and evaporates as it ages, so if the barrel were taxed on the volume of its contents straight off the still, distillers would be paying for bourbon that was essentially disappearing into thin air.

As a solution, the government created bonded warehouses. These were essentially government-observed rickhouses where distillers could age their spirits for a set period (initially a year) before taxation set in. To keep up with the stock, the federal government split states into taxation districts. Before Prohibition, there were eight of these districts, starting with District 1 in Western Kentucky and moving sequentially across the state to District 8 in its far eastern tip. Within those districts, each distillery—and the stills it housed—was registered as a "distilled spirits plant" and numbered. (Think of it like numbering schools in a school district.) While the numbering system was initially pretty simple, big cultural developments like Prohibition and distillery acquisitions and consolidations have shaken things up throughout the years. Additionally, Kentucky did away with the taxation districts in the 1990s and took a statewide approach to recording and monitoring new distilleries and stills.

Today, the system remains in place for the same reason it did in the Civil War era: to keep up with taxation. Here are the DSP numbers for some of the best-known brands in Kentucky:

**FOUR ROSES DISTILLERY:** DSP-KY-8, DSP-KY-62

**HEAVEN HILL DISTILLERY:** DSP-KY-1, DSP-KY-31

**MAKER'S MARK DISTILLERY:** DSP-KY-44

**STITZEL-WELLER DISTILLERY:** DSP-KY-16

**WOODFORD RESERVE DISTILLERY:** DSP-KY-52

## "Kentucky Straight Bourbon"

This label designation is simple. While bourbon can be made anywhere in the United States, only bourbon produced in Kentucky can be labeled "Kentucky Straight Bourbon." And in my humble opinion, it's the best-quality bourbon in the country—for now. There are bourbon distilleries in other states as far-flung as Texas, Colorado, Utah, and Virginia, and many are starting to make quality bourbon. Kentucky just happened to have a two-hundred-year head start.

## Unregulated Terms

While there are numerous legal regulations for what a distiller has to do in order for a product to be classified as bourbon on the shelf, there are terms you may see on a bottle that are *not* federally regulated. Instead, these are merely descriptive terms used for marketing.

For instance, the phrase "small batch" is not federally regulated; a producer can put that on a bottle whether they make two barrels of bourbon or twenty thousand. Similarly, terms like "all natural," "handcrafted," and "vintage" are unregulated. Many buyers assume that the "single barrel" designation, which denotes that a bottle's contents came from one bourbon barrel rather than a mixture of batches, is federally overseen, but this is not the case.

# THE I-65 SOUTH CORRIDOR

This is probably the most popular route of the major bourbon tours you can take in Kentucky. It will lead you through some of the most historic landmarks in bourbon, and some newer ones, too. Distilleries in Kentucky are spread out, and visiting them requires long hours of driving. Depending on how long you linger at each, you may only do two distillery visits in a day, or you could be ambitious and hit every distillery along this route. The choice is completely up to you.

Starting in Louisville, take I-65 South and then turn down some winding country roads toward Bardstown. If you're planning a day of bourbon tasting, you're going to need a strong breakfast, so take a quick detour through Valley Station to Christi's Café and scarf down a hefty chicken-fried steak breakfast while Dolly Parton plays on the jukebox. Then, with a full stomach, head toward Clermont on the outskirts of Bernheim Arboretum and Research Forest, meandering past pristine black rickhouses and up a small country road to the headquarters of **JIM BEAM DISTILLERY**, home of master distiller Fred Noe and the generations of distillers before him who make up one of the most historic families of bourbon. It's a vast campus with long winding paths, and columns of steam

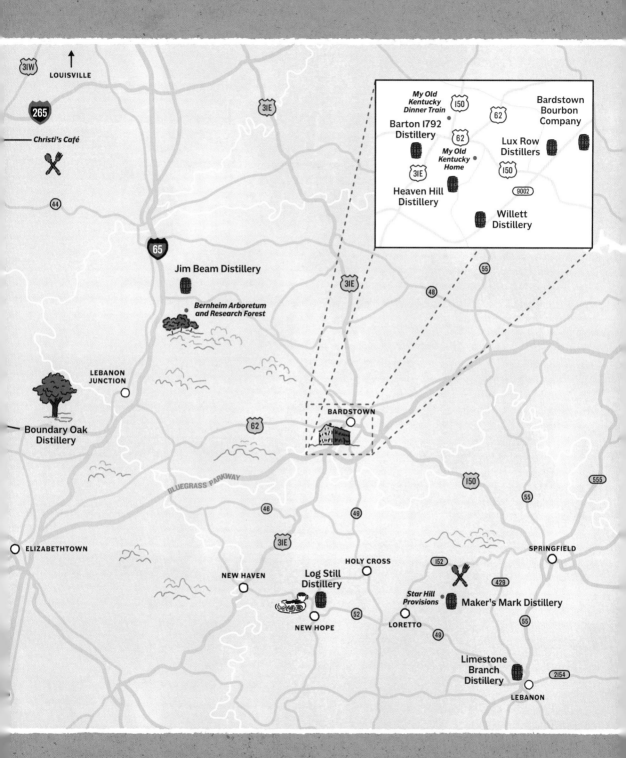

31W

↑ LOUISVILLE

265

Christi's Café

44

**Jim Beam Distillery**

*Bernheim Arboretum and Research Forest*

65

LEBANON JUNCTION

**Boundary Oak Distillery**

31E

48

55

31E

BARDSTOWN

62

BLUEGRASS PARKWAY

46

49

150

55

555

55

ELIZABETHTOWN

31E

HOLY CROSS

SPRINGFIELD

NEW HAVEN

**Log Still Distillery**

152

429

*Star Hill Provisions*

**Maker's Mark Distillery**

NEW HOPE

52

LORETTO

49

55

**Limestone Branch Distillery**

2154

LEBANON

*My Old Kentucky Dinner Train*

150

62

**Bardstown Bourbon Company**

**Barton 1792 Distillery**

62

**Lux Row Distillers**

31E

*My Old Kentucky Home*

150

9002

**Heaven Hill Distillery**

**Willett Distillery**

coming from the boilers blanket the grounds in the sweet smell of cooking corn.

Afterward, head south on I-65 until you come to the heart of bourbon: Bardstown, Kentucky, one of the coolest small towns in America. Named after William and David Bard, who founded the town in 1788 from a land grant in what was once Virginia, Bardstown is now home to the largest, loudest, most raucous bourbon festival in the world, held every September. It's also home to the Oscar Getz Museum of Whiskey History, a must-stop for bourbon aficionados. And yes, this is also the place where you can't walk a mile without running into some of the best bourbon distilleries in Kentucky.

Start at **WILLETT DISTILLERY**, makers of esteemed bourbons such as Noah's Mill and Willett Pot Still Reserve. You might run into Willett's master distiller, Drew Kulsveen, who will walk you around the pastoral grounds and rustic rickhouses. Don't miss the bar here for a world-class cocktail and some of the best bites of food you'll have all afternoon.

From here, take a short drive to **HEAVEN HILL DISTILLERY**, one of the most historic and important distilleries in the ongoing story of bourbon. Founded in 1935, Heaven Hill is overseen by master distiller Conor O'Driscoll, who is responsible for some of the most delicious bourbons on the market. Spend some time here, because this is history you want to absorb as if by osmosis.

Bourbon is dominated by big brands, but today, craft distilleries are making waves in the industry, and you'll find some of the best of them in and around Bardstown. One notable example is **BOUNDARY OAK DISTILLERY**, which is located at the base of a hundred-year-old oak tree where the naturally found spring water is used to distill their bourbon. **LIMESTONE BRANCH DISTILLERY** is at the forefront of the craft distillery movement. The owners come from the pedigree of Jim Beam so they know what they are talking about, and their Yellowstone Select bourbon is flying off shelves all over the country.

**LUX ROW DISTILLERS** may look like a brand-spanking-new distillery, and it is, but the company actually has a long history with labels like Ezra Brooks and David Nicholson. The bourbon boom has inspired companies that were previously doing contract distilling—making bourbons for other labels—to open their own facilities, which only makes the end product better. **LOG STILL DISTILLERY** is a special place that blends tradition with a modern vision of what a distillery can do when combined with a beautiful restaurant, a bed-and-breakfast, an amphitheater for musical acts, and all-around Southern hospitality. In contrast to the new wave of craft distillers is **BARTON 1792 DISTILLERY**, the oldest-running distillery in Bardstown, which can boast of its origins back in 1879. With age comes knowledge, and there's a reason

Barton's high rye bourbon keeps winning awards, so it would behoove you to stop in and see what happens when tradition is allowed to flourish. All these distilleries follow the same rules for bourbon making, but each one has a different heritage, and it's important to see them all. And while you're in Bardstown, consider having a meal at My Old Kentucky Dinner Train. You might think you're too cool for a tourist trap, but where else can you have a fancy dinner on a moving train after a day of tasting bourbon?

Slightly off the beaten path, you'll find a fascinating operation at **BARDSTOWN BOURBON COMPANY**. This is a modern contract distillery, which means it doesn't have its own label but it makes the juice for some of the best bottles in the world. Their products are sleek, efficient, and delicious. This just may be the future of bourbon distilling.

Venture farther south on I-65 along curving pastoral roads that take you through rolling hills where you may have to stop for wild turkeys in the middle of the road. You'll wind up at one of the meccas of bourbon— **MAKER'S MARK DISTILLERY**—a place where time moves slower and conversations happen friendlier, and bourbon history is everywhere. Slow down, enjoy the architecture, and have a meal at Star Hill Provisions. Your afternoon will pass in a dreamy landscape that seems like it was touched by angels.

# BACON CORN PONE
# WITH BOURBON ONION JAM

Corn pone is a version of cornbread that is usually cooked like a free-form pancake. The flavor of char is essential in this recipe. A little is pleasurable, smoky, intense, like the flavor of bourbon itself. Too much becomes offensive. The batter for this savory pancake hits the perfect balance when fried to a crispy brown, with the taste of smoky bacon inside and bourbon-infused jam on top.

**Makes 8 to 10 discs, each about 2 inches in diameter**

3 slices bacon, chopped

¾ cup cornmeal

¼ cup all-purpose flour

1½ teaspoons baking powder

¼ teaspoon baking soda

½ cup buttermilk

I teaspoon sugar

¼ teaspoon kosher salt

Bourbon Onion Jam (recipe follows), for serving

Heat a large skillet over high heat and add the bacon. Cook, stirring often, until crispy, 3 to 5 minutes. Remove the bacon from the pan and drain on a paper towel. Leave the bacon fat in the pan over low heat while you make the batter.

In a large bowl, mix the cornmeal, flour, baking powder, and baking soda thoroughly with a fork. Add the buttermilk, sugar, and salt and mix until thoroughly combined. Fold in the fried bacon.

Raise the heat under the skillet of bacon fat to medium. When the fat is hot, add about 2 tablespoons of the batter in a mound for each corn pone; you should be able to fit 4 in the pan. Fry for 2 to 3 minutes per side, until very lightly charred. Remove from the pan and drain on paper towels. (You can transfer them to a baking sheet and let them sit in a warm oven while you cook the rest, if you like.) Repeat with the remaining batter.

To serve, top each corn pone with a little bourbon onion jam and serve warm.

# BOURBON ONION JAM

The earthy sweetness of slow-caramelized onions, dripping with umami, is mirrored in the characteristics of a bourbon that is gently reduced to a syrupy consistency. I could live on this jam. Make a double batch and enjoy it on everything from Bacon Corn Pone (opposite) to a cheese plate, or use it as a topping for a burger or even a pizza.

### Makes 1 cup

2 teaspoons olive oil

1½ pounds sweet onions, diced

1 cup bourbon

¼ cup pure maple syrup

¼ cup soy sauce

2 tablespoons apple cider vinegar

1½ teaspoons kosher salt

½ teaspoon red pepper flakes

In a medium pot, heat the olive oil over medium heat. Add the onions and cook, stirring frequently with a wooden spoon, for about 12 minutes, until the onions are translucent and starting to caramelize. Add the bourbon, maple syrup, soy sauce, and vinegar to the pot. Cook, stirring and scraping up any browned bits from the bottom of the pan, until the mixture starts to thicken, about 25 minutes.

Add the salt and red pepper flakes and cook until most of the liquid has cooked off, about 5 minutes more. Transfer the onion jam to a glass jar and let cool to room temperature, then cover and store in the fridge for up to 2 weeks.

# FRIED HALLOUMI CHEESE WITH SPICED BOURBON HONEY

Halloumi is generally an unripened goat's- and sheep's-milk cheese that has a high melting point, so it can withstand a good, hard sear. It's salty but a bit bland. Adding bourbon harmonizes with the salty squeak of the cheese and the sweet spiced honey in this recipe. Don't be afraid to use more bourbon than the recipe calls for. Because in this case, the more is, definitely, the merrier.

**Serves 4 as a snack or 2 as an appetizer**

### FOR THE BOURBON HONEY

6 tablespoons honey

½ cup bourbon, reduced to ¼ cup (see page 75)

1½ teaspoons fresh lemon juice

⅛ teaspoon smoked paprika

Kosher salt and freshly ground black pepper

### FOR THE CHEESE

8 ounces Halloumi cheese, cut into ½-inch-thick slices (about 8 slices)

2 teaspoons olive oil

2 slices sourdough bread, cut into 8 small squares total

1 teaspoon fresh thyme

To make the bourbon honey, in a small bowl, combine the honey, reduced bourbon, lemon juice, paprika, and salt and pepper to taste and whisk with a fork to combine.

To prepare the cheese, place the Halloumi in a large bowl and pour half the bourbon honey over it. Set aside to marinate for about 1 hour.

In a large skillet, heat 1 teaspoon of the olive oil over high heat. Add the bread pieces and toast for 1 minute. Transfer to a plate.

Add the remaining 1 teaspoon olive oil to the skillet. Remove the Halloumi from the bourbon honey, letting the liquid drain back into the bowl, and pat dry. Add the cheese to the pan and sear for about 1 minute, until nicely caramelized on the bottom, then flip and cook on the second side for 1 minute, or until caramelized.

Place the fried cheese over the toasted bread and drizzle with the remaining bourbon honey. Top with the thyme and serve right away.

# ROASTED FENNEL AND BOURBON–BURNT ORANGE SALAD

Fennel is typically lauded for its bright, fresh anise notes, but it takes on an entirely different identity after it undergoes an intense roast. Slow-roasted notes take over where the anise turns to sweetness. The orange caramelizes and the bourbon dominates. This is a texturally rich, hearty salad in which the brightness of the fennel tabbouleh balances out the charred notes.

**Serves 2**

2 heads fennel

2 tablespoons olive oil

Kosher salt and freshly ground
    black pepper

1 Roma (plum) tomato, finely chopped

½ cup fresh mint, finely chopped

2 garlic cloves, minced

1 tablespoon fresh lemon juice

Zest of 1 orange

¼ teaspoon ground cumin

3 oranges

1½ teaspoons sugar

2 tablespoons bourbon

3 ounces crumbled feta cheese

Preheat the oven to 400°F.

Cut the long stems from the fennel bulb and set aside. Cut the bulb in half through the core, then remove the core with a sharp paring knife and discard. Cut each half of the fennel bulb into 4 equal slices. Toss the fennel in a bowl with 1½ tablespoons of the olive oil, and salt and pepper to taste. Transfer the fennel to a sheet pan in a single layer and roast for 25 minutes, or until the edges have browned and softened.

Meanwhile, remove the fronds from the fennel stems and finely chop them; you'll need ½ cup. Finely chop the fennel stems as well; you'll need 1 cup. Combine the chopped stems and fronds in a bowl with the tomato, mint, garlic, lemon juice, orange zest, and cumin. Mix thoroughly and season with salt and pepper. Set aside until ready to serve.

**« CONTINUED »**

Remove the roasted fennel from the oven and let cool to room temperature.

Cut the oranges into wheels and remove the skin and pith from each. Arrange the slices on a plate and sprinkle the tops with sugar.

In a large skillet, heat the remaining ½ tablespoon olive oil over high heat. Add the oranges to the pan, sugared-side down, and sear for about 3 minutes, until the oranges are caramelized on the bottom. Turn off the heat. Add the bourbon to the pan and deglaze the pan for 1 minute.

Divide the orange slices between two plates, with the caramelized side facing up. Top with the roasted fennel and the fennel-tomato mixture. Finish with the crumbled feta. Serve right away.

# HOW TO REDUCE BOURBON

In order to reduce bourbon quickly and safely, you will need a large (4-quart) pot with a tight-fitting lid (for smaller quantities, use a high-sided small or medium saucepan with a tight-fitting lid). Pour 2 cups bourbon into the pot and set it over high heat. The ethanol in the bourbon will ignite, so do not hold your face or hands anywhere near the top of the pot. When the bourbon ignites, reduce the heat to medium-low and cover the pot with the lid. The lack of oxygen will tamp out the flame. After a few seconds, remove the lid; this will reintroduce oxygen to the ethanol, so it will most likely reignite, but the flame will be smaller and more controlled. Cover the pot partially with the lid and cook until the bourbon has reduced by half. At this point, most of the ethanol will have burned off and you will be left with a liquid with concentrated bourbon flavor and minimal alcohol. Reduced bourbon can be stored in a jar or in the original bottle at room temperature for several months.

# BEEF TARTARE ON BURNT OAK PLANKS

I've been serving a dish similar to this at my restaurant, 610 Magnolia, for over a decade. It's not tartare in the French style, but a miso-sesame-rich, umami-forward version of tartare. The oak planks you need to flavor the beef are not difficult to find; any hardware store will have them and cut them for you. The extra step of burning the wood and serving the tartare directly on the planks is what makes this dish extra special. It is elegant and fragrant, and it reinforces the idea of the charred oak barrels where your bourbon aged. Every time you dip your fork against the wood, the slightest trace of charred oak will mix with the tartare, flavoring each bite.

**Serves 2 as an appetizer**

**FOR THE MARINADE**

½ cup bourbon, reduced to 2 tablespoons (see page 75)

2 tablespoons ketchup

1 tablespoon dark miso paste

1 tablespoon apple cider vinegar

1½ teaspoons soy sauce

1½ teaspoons toasted sesame oil

1½ teaspoons brown sugar

¼ teaspoon paprika

**FOR THE TARTARE**

6 ounces beef (filet mignon or eye of round)

1 tablespoon finely chopped shallot

1 teaspoon bourbon

2 tablespoons finely chopped fresh chives

Bourbon Salt (recipe follows)

Olive oil, for garnish

**SPECIAL EQUIPMENT**

2 (6-inch) square oak wood planks

To make the marinade, in a small bowl, stir together the reduced bourbon, ketchup, miso, vinegar, soy sauce, sesame oil, brown sugar, and paprika.

To prepare the tartare, thinly slice the beef against the grain, then finely chop it until it resembles coarse ground beef. Transfer the chopped beef to a bowl and add the shallot and the marinade. Let marinate in the fridge for 20 minutes.

Take the oak wood planks and wipe the bourbon over them with a cloth. Set a gas burner to high or heat a grill to high. For each plank, hold the wood with tongs and place it directly over the fire on one of the flat sides until you get an even char over the entire surface. This may take some time, but be patient with it. Place the plank charred-side up on a sheet pan to cool before serving; the wood should be room temperature when you serve the tartare.

Set a 3-inch ring mold on the charred wood plank, then add a thin layer of the beef tartare; repeat with the second plank. Garnish with the chives. Top with a sprinkle of bourbon salt and a light drizzle of olive oil just before serving.

# BOURBON SALT

You'll be surprised at how easy bourbon salt is to make and how much flavor bourbon infuses into sea salt. This may become your everyday salt; you can use it to lend its intensity to everything from steaks to salads, even ice cream.

### Makes 1 cup

2½ cups bourbon                                    1 cup coarse sea salt

Preheat the oven to 200°F. Line a sheet pan with parchment paper.

In a medium pot, bring the bourbon to a simmer over medium heat (see page 75). Cook until it has reduced by half, about 10 minutes. Add the salt to the pot and simmer for 5 minutes more, or until most of the bourbon has been cooked off.

Spread the wet salt over the prepared pan in a thin layer. Bake until the salt is dry but not burned, about 1 hour. Let cool to room temperature. Store in an airtight container at room temperature for up to a month.

# BONE-IN PORK CHOPS IN BOURBON MARINADE WITH BOURBON WHOLE-GRAIN MUSTARD SAUCE

When bourbon is utilized in a marinade, it has a twofold purpose: It not only adds flavor to the meat, but it also helps to tenderize it. This recipe doubles down on the bourbon in the marinade by accompanying the pork with a sharp bourbon-fortified mustard sauce. The two bourbons react differently in the dish: one disappearing as a back note in the marinade, and the other punching you on the nose up front.

**Serves 2 as a main**

### FOR THE MARINADE

1 cup bourbon, reduced to ¼ cup
  (see page 75)

2 tablespoons soy sauce

1 tablespoon Worcestershire sauce

1 tablespoon brown sugar

2 garlic cloves, minced

### FOR THE PORK CHOPS

2 (12-ounce) pork chops

1 tablespoon olive oil

2 tablespoons unsalted butter

1 cup shiitake mushrooms, halved

2 garlic cloves, minced

1 shallot, coarsely chopped

1 cup Brussels sprout leaves

### FOR THE BOURBON WHOLE-GRAIN MUSTARD SAUCE

½ cup bourbon

1 cup chicken stock

¼ cup heavy cream

3 tablespoons whole-grain mustard

Kosher salt and freshly ground
  black pepper

Preheat the oven to 350°F.

To make the marinade, in a large zip-top bag, combine the reduced bourbon, soy sauce, Worcestershire, brown sugar, and garlic. Seal the bag, give it a toss to mix it, and add the pork chops. Reseal the bag, getting out as much air as possible. Place the bag on a plate and marinate in the fridge for at least 10 hours or up to overnight.

**« CONTINUED »**

To prepare the pork chops, when you're ready to cook them, remove them from the marinade and pat dry with paper towels. Discard the marinade.

In a large skillet, heat the olive oil over medium-high heat. When the oil is hot, add the pork chops and cook for 4 minutes on each side, until nicely browned on both sides. Transfer the pork chops to a sheet pan. Let the pork chops finish cooking in the oven for 10 to 12 minutes, until fully cooked through but still moist in the middle.

Meanwhile, clean out the skillet with a paper towel and place over medium-high heat. Add the butter. When it foams, add the mushrooms, garlic, and shallot. Cook for 2 minutes. Add the Brussels sprout leaves and cook for 1 minute. Transfer all the vegetables from the skillet to the sheet pan with the pork chops.

To make the bourbon whole-grain mustard sauce, return the skillet to high heat. Deglaze the pan with the bourbon. Cook until the bourbon is almost all gone, scraping the bottom of the pan to lift any caramelized bits. Add the stock and boil for 3 minutes, or until the stock reduces by a third. Add the cream and cook for 2 minutes more, then turn off the heat and whisk in the mustard. Season with salt and pepper.

Transfer the pork chops to a platter. Spoon some vegetables on top of the pork chops. Spoon the sauce around the pork chops and serve right away.

# CHARRED RIB EYE STEAK
# WITH BOURBON-SOY BUTTER

Beef, bourbon, and soy sauce are essential flavors for me. In this recipe, the steak is charred for smokiness. The soy sauce adds richness and salinity. The bourbon adds age and notes of caramel. The culinary trinity is bridged by the butter. As the compound butter melts over the warm singed skin of the steak, the marriage of these three flavors is simple yet sublime.

**Serves 2 as a main**

**FOR THE BOURBON-SOY BUTTER**

1 cup bourbon

¼ cup soy sauce

3 tablespoons sugar

1 tablespoon toasted sesame oil

3 garlic cloves, grated on a Microplane

1 pound (4 sticks) unsalted butter, at room temperature

**FOR THE STEAK**

1 (14-ounce) rib eye steak

Kosher salt and freshly ground black pepper

2 tablespoons clarified butter

6 garlic cloves, peeled

Fresh horseradish, for grating

To make the bourbon-soy butter, pour the bourbon into a small pot and simmer over medium heat until reduced by half. Add the soy sauce, sugar, sesame oil, and garlic. Bring the mixture back to a simmer, then transfer it to a small bowl and let cool until just slightly warm to the touch.

Place the butter in a large bowl. Drizzle in the warm liquid a little at a time and use a whisk to combine with the butter. When all the liquid has been incorporated into the butter, transfer it to a lidded container or roll it into 1½-inch-thick logs and wrap in plastic wrap. Chill the butter in the fridge for at least 1 hour before using. Make sure to bring it back to room temperature before serving.

To cook the steak, season it generously with salt and pepper. Heat a cast-iron pan over medium-high heat and add the clarified butter. Add the steak to the pan. Cook for 4 minutes, until the steak is seared and browned on the bottom. Using tongs, hold the steak on its edge and cook until browned, then turn so that all the edges are nicely browned. Flip the steak to the other side and sear for 4 minutes. Meanwhile, add the garlic cloves to the pan to cook alongside the steak. Baste the steak with the clarified butter and garlic for 3 to 6 minutes, until the meat is medium-rare (for medium doneness, cook for 2 minutes more on each side; cooking to well-done is not recommended for this steak). Remove the steak from the pan and let it rest on a cutting board for 2 minutes. Remove the garlic cloves as well; they should be browned but soft in the middle.

Slice the steak and place it on a warm plate. Serve with the cooked garlic cloves and a spoonful or slice of the bourbon-soy butter over the steak. Grate fresh horseradish over the steak just before serving. The butter should melt over the steak, but if the meat isn't warm enough, put the entire plate in a 250°F oven for 3 minutes and then serve right away.

Store the leftover bourbon-soy butter in the refrigerator for up to a month to use on steaks, roasted vegetables, or fried eggs.

# CORN AND LEATHER

Much of the land in the Kentuckiana (Kentucky + Indiana) region offers an abundance of flat, fertile earth ideal for growing commodity crops. You can drive along highways in Indiana, Ohio, and Kentucky and find endless miles of corn, soybean, and wheat farms. Tobacco farms used to be prevalent in Kentucky, but not anymore. They've given way to fields of corn stretching as far as the eye can see. They are jungles of monotony. They are greedy for sunlight. This is field corn or feed corn. Much of it goes to feed hogs and chickens. A bunch of it is used to make ethanol for fuel. And only the best of it goes into making bourbon.

Field corn is not the same as sweet corn. These are not the bright yellow ears bursting with sweet kernels that you find at the farmers' market. Field corn is tough. It's hard and crusty. At harvest, the kernels are ripped from the ears and stored in silos all through autumn and winter. The individual kernels feel like leather, and they fall into your mouth like pebbles. They're high in starch, so when you pop one between your teeth, you get a distinct taste of corn powder, not the creamy milk of sweet corn. Take a handful of dried grits right out of the package and shove them in your mouth. That will give you an idea of what field corn tastes like after harvest.

Versailles, Kentucky, has one of the few non-GMO cornfields grown specifically for the bourbon industry. This is a flat, treeless plot of land. In the middle of summer, the heat is unbearable and the sunlight is deafening. But the temperature doesn't bother Hoppy Henton. He runs this farm, which was started by his great-great-grandfather, who farmed tobacco and livestock. He himself has grown tobacco and wheat and produce and raised livestock. He's been focusing mostly on field corn since the mid-1990s.

Corn is planted in rows so tight that it's near impossible to walk between the stalks. Hoppy calls each ear of corn a miracle. He explains that the tassels on the top of each cornstalk release pollen, which must be picked up by the silks on the lower stalk. Each silk is responsible for a single row of kernels.

If you see an ear of corn that's missing a row of kernels, that one missed a fleck of pollen. As the pollen falls, it's picked up by the smallest movement of air and pollinates the silks. There's not much of a breeze in the valley where Versailles is situated, so the closer the cornstalks are to one another, the better the chance the pollen has to fertilize the stigma. At the middle of Hoppy's cornfield, it is dense and shadowy. There's no movement, barely any air, and the blades of the cornstalk leaves are sharp as knives. But this is where Hoppy goes to inspect his crop. "You can't tell a crop by the edges," he says.

Most of Hoppy's fields are planted with DeKalb or Pioneer seed, though he's got some experimental blocks of land growing newer strains. Most of his corn will be harvested to make bourbon. The corn will be dried and ground and fermented with yeast to make the mash that will be distilled into the corn whiskey that turns into bourbon. He plants about thirty thousand stalks per acre in April and harvests in mid-September. The corn is dried for about a week to about 14 percent moisture. Some of the harvest is hauled out immediately and the rest stays in grain bins until it's needed, since bourbon is made all year round. He can store up to thirty thousand bushels of dried corn in his silos.

Like most farmers, Hoppy is a quiet, confident man who has seen the ups and downs of the farming life. He remembers the lean years. Any time I ask him something he doesn't agree with, he'll tell me it's poppycock. Like when I ask him if organic corn makes bourbon taste better. He stands tall and straight, not unlike a giant stalk of corn. His hands are large and strong, with gnarled fingers that look like ears of corn glued onto a palm. He's what we would call an old-fashioned man, unimpressed by the modern machinations of farming and technology. But he is quick to defend his non-GMO corn. He tells me that once you put the corn through the distillation process, there's no way to test the final product to see if it was made with GMO or non-GMO corn. "It's just an integrity thing for me. They turn my little crop into something a thousand times more valuable than what I can sell it for," says Hoppy. By "they," he means the bourbon industry, which produces coveted bottles of bourbon that get shipped out to the fanciest and trendiest bars and restaurants across America.

Hoppy takes pride in knowing he can connect the dots between his corn, the bourbon bottles he sees for sale, and his land in Kentucky. I think about this a lot, too, when I'm in some newfangled speakeasy in a modern city with crowds

of merrymakers drinking a bourbon cocktail with passion fruit gel or a botanical shrub. I look inside the bottle of bourbon for that familiar golden-brown water that brings me back to fields in Kentucky, and I marvel at the journey and the people who are connected to this liquid. From the farmer to the distiller to the bartender to the enthusiast. All from a kernel of corn. I think about Hoppy a lot. I think about what he told me when I asked him how much bourbon he drinks: "Always one, sometimes two, never three." I think about the slow yet forceful way he walks through his farm, nurturing his cornstalks so they will properly mature into perfect yellow ears of corn destined to be distilled.

And what, exactly, happens to that corn? My investigation is about the flavor of bourbon, and the thing that mystifies me is the transformation from corn kernel to bourbon. When corn is fermented and distilled, the clear alcohol that comes off the still is called white dog or white lightning or moonshine. This unaged distillate is so sweet, it makes your teeth hurt; it's reminiscent of candy corn and shoots through your insides like a jolt of fire. You can smell and taste the corn—it is pure and fragrant. All that starch in the field corn has been converted to alcohol, resulting in a high-proof liquid with a distinct corn flavor. But it's not bourbon. It's not even whiskey. Something happens to that corn flavor during aging. The resulting brown bourbon tastes nothing like the white dog. The corn mellows, dissipates, transforms into what I cannot clearly identify. It could be the dried fruit flavor, the leather, the hay, the dried grass notes that I love about bourbon. It could be the soft, sweet notes lurking around the corners of each sip. It's impossible to pinpoint what, exactly, the corn flavor develops into after years in a barrel. There's a quality in bourbon that is like dried fruit and sweet, but bitter and deep at the same time. I can only describe it as fruit leather. It feels like the corn reincarnated as leather packed with dark, sweet fruit. Hoppy tells me there's no way for sure to say what happens to the corn flavor since there are so many other variables that go into making bourbon. He says, "Rye gives you spicy flavor; barley has some starch but more sweetness. You can put anything in a barrel and it'll come out looking brown. Corn is the magical part of it."

So much about bourbon is still unexplainable. Bourbon has gone from backyard stills to multimillion-dollar distilleries using the latest science and technology, but there's still a mystery to it, a romance. There are some in the whiskey world who will tell you that corn is just a high-starch crop that was convenient for making whiskey because it was plentiful at a time when cheap whiskey was needed. That it's no more important to the process than the water or the yeast. But there are others who walk the plains of Kentucky and see a vision of the past, where an unbelievable confluence of history gave rise to bourbon—the corn, yes, but also the oak trees that were here in Kentucky that just happened to be perfect for barrel making, the limestone-rich waters, the hot summers and cold winters, the Ohio River that flowed into the Mississippi, where whiskey was sent on slow-moving boats to New Orleans. If that isn't magic, I don't know what is.

# WHY CORN IS USED
# IN BOURBON

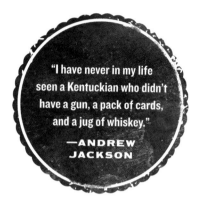

"I have never in my life seen a Kentuckian who didn't have a gun, a pack of cards, and a jug of whiskey."
—ANDREW JACKSON

Kentucky is part of America's Corn Belt, a region where corn grows particularly well thanks to the state's rich soil, well-distributed rainfall, and unique geography. The region's original residents were Native American tribes, including the Cherokee and Piqua Shawnee, skilled farmers and cultivators who revered corn as a crop. Corn was often celebrated through green corn ceremonies, and festivals were held by Native growers hoping for a fruitful harvest.

European farmers who settled in Kentucky eventually came to use corn as an ingredient not only in their meals but also in their spirits. When farmers first settled in Kentucky, there were no regulations for what went into the whiskey that would later become bourbon. Corn was simply cheap and plentiful in the region, so it made sense that they would plant it and distill any extra grain into a spirit they could sell during the off-season.

But the practice wasn't wholly developed out of necessity. Remember that whiskey was made from such varied crops as wheat, barley, apples, carrots—basically anything that would ferment in a still. Corn is high in starch, which means that once it's cooked, it converts to a high-sugar mash. The more sugar in the mash, the more alcohol is created in the fermentation process. And corn created a sweet-tasting, smooth flavor that relaxed the harsher notes of the wheat, barley, and rye that were typically used in American whiskeys.

Even today, the novice whiskey drinker will gravitate toward bourbon over rye or Canadian whiskey. It is as appealing a libation now as it was in the 1800s.

According to historian Michael Veach, James C. Crow was one of the first distillers to perfect a corn-heavy whiskey mash bill at the Old Oscar Pepper Distillery. His recipe was such a success that it inspired many imitators, and corn-based whiskey in Kentucky was off to the races. In 1909, President William Taft issued the "Taft Decision," stipulating that bourbon whiskey must have a majority corn mash bill, and in 1935, the Standards of Identity for Distilled Spirits—part of the US Code of Federal Regulations—mandated that bourbon must include 51 percent corn in the mash bill.

Today, it is estimated that the state of Kentucky will grind, ferment, and distill about 20 million bushels of corn for the bourbon industry. That means bourbon is using more corn than any other industry in the state, including feed for livestock, fuel for ethanol, and, of course, food for the dinner table.

# BEYOND CORN: WHEAT, RYE, BARLEY, AND MALT

Throughout most of America's whiskey history, four grains have been predominantly used in whiskey making: corn, wheat, rye, and barley. We know that bourbon, by law, has to be at least 51 percent corn, but what about the rest of the mash bill? If you've ever tasted 100 percent corn whiskey, you know that just because a majority-corn mash bill is delicious doesn't mean you can go all the way with it. Bourbon needs spice and structure and bitterness to balance out the sweet corn. Each grain adds something to the bourbon, and consumers can decide which flavors they enjoy best. Here are the basics on the grains used alongside corn in bourbon.

## Wheat

Have you ever heard a bourbon referred to as smooth? It was probably wheat dominant. Many bourbons contain some wheat in their mash bill, but having a high percentage of wheat will give bourbon a distinctive flavor. Filled with honey, vanilla, dried berries, spice, and toffee flavors, wheat whiskeys tend to be mellow, smooth, and soft.

## Rye

If wheat equals smoothness, rye contributes notes of spice to bourbon. Rye-dominant bourbons and whiskeys tend to have really lovely peppercorn notes, tobacco scents, and roasted nut flavors. In fact, rye is so popular a flavor that there is a major push to make 100 percent rye whiskeys in many bourbon distilleries. Rye whiskey is not bourbon per se, but many bourbon lovers enjoy the bite and spice of this whiskey, which was prominent in America before the advent of corn.

## Barley and Malt

Barley, especially malted barley, adds an earthiness to bourbon. As it is technically a cereal grain, there can be a definite "cereal" wheat note present, as well as flavors like brown sugar, smoke, and chocolate. Barley has traditionally been used sparingly in bourbon recipes, but as times change, so do tastes. There are increasing numbers of experimental bourbons with high-barley mash bills. Malted barley is a process that allows the barley to produce enzymes that make the grain much more amenable to fermentation. It also adds a nutty flavor to the bourbon that has proven to be popular with whiskey drinkers.

For decades, mash bills were a combination of just these three grains, plus corn—which, of course, makes up at least 51 percent of the bourbon mash bill. However, in 2019, the Alcohol and Tobacco Tax and Trade Bureau (TTB) made the decision to allow a limited subset of additional grains to be included in the whiskey mash bill. These include, per the organization, "cereal grains and the seeds of the pseudocereals amaranth, buckwheat, and quinoa."

This rule has opened up a new world of innovation for whiskey distillers. For example, Corsair Distillery in Nashville, Tennessee, released a quinoa whiskey made using quinoa and malted barley; KOVAL in Chicago, Illinois, released a single-barrel oat whiskey; and Buffalo Trace released the sought-after Colonel E. H. Taylor "Amaranth Grain of the Gods" Straight Kentucky Bourbon Whiskey.

# BOULEVARDIER

The boulevardier is one of the most classic cocktails in the bourbon canon and Dante Wheat Jr. is one of the most classic bartenders. His creations, like this cocktail, are precise yet imbued with artistry.

**Makes I**

I¼ ounces wheated bourbon
(see page 32)

¾ ounce sweet vermouth, preferably
Carpano Antica Formula

¾ ounce Campari

I orange peel

In a mixing glass, combine the bourbon, vermouth, and Campari. Add ice and stir until the glass is cold to the touch. Strain into a double old-fashioned glass over a large ice cube. Express the orange peel over the glass, then use it as a garnish.

"Bourbon whiskey is Kentucky's greatest art medium. Each barrel is a handcrafted piece, showing our home to the world."
—DANTE WHEAT JR.

# THE NAMES
# BEHIND THE LABELS

Walk through the bourbon aisle of a liquor store, and you'll notice that bourbon brands, more than any other spirit, are named after historical figures. Who are these people? What is their connection to bourbon? If you look them up, you'll learn a great deal about the history of bourbon, and of Kentucky. These notable names were the founders of the bourbon industry, and while many details of their lives have been lost to history, they live on in the bottles that carry their legacies.

## Albert B. Blanton

Colonel Albert B. Blanton joined Buffalo Trace back in 1897, when it was still known as the George T. Stagg Distillery. In 1921, he was promoted to president of the distillery and managed to help keep the business afloat during Prohibition by obtaining a "medical whiskey" license. He steered the ship through the rough waters of the Great Depression and World War II, and his ingenuity and creativity in the face of adversity have inspired many contemporary distillers—it's no surprise that Buffalo Trace's premier single-barrel bourbon is named after him.

## Elmer T. Lee

Elmer T. Lee worked at Buffalo Trace during Albert B. Blanton's tenure as president—but not without some initial difficulty. When he first applied to work at the distillery, Blanton himself told Lee they weren't hiring. However, Lee was a World War II veteran with an engineering degree, so he eventually scored a job as a maintenance engineer. He cycled through a variety of jobs—including plant engineer and plant manager—before finally becoming the distillery's very first master distiller. In 1984, he was the first distiller to introduce a single-barrel bourbon to market.

## E. H. Taylor

Colonel Edmund Haynes Taylor was a driving force behind the modernization of bourbon as we know it. He popularized copper fermentation tanks, column stills, and contemporary rickhouses, and he was one of the biggest proponents of the Bottled-in-Bond Act of 1897 (see page 57), one of the first major moves toward consumer protection in the spirits industry.

## Pappy Van Winkle

When many people think "expensive bourbon," they likely think of Pappy Van Winkle (and the infamous "Pappygate" heist of 2013 that saw $100,000 of it stolen from Buffalo Trace). The real Pappy, Julian P. Van Winkle Sr., was a pioneer of wheated bourbon and was fanatical about his pursuit of exceptional flavor, texture, and character in America's native spirit.

## Elijah Craig

Elijah Craig was a Baptist preacher who is sometimes credited with the invention of American bourbon. In 1789, he was the first distiller to age his whiskey in new charred oak barrels. Some claim that an accidental fire charred his barrels and changed the whiskey inside. Others say he stored his whiskey in former sugar barrels that were then charred and was impressed with how charring improved the flavor. Over his life, he continued perfecting the barrel-charring process, which is now a required element of bourbon production.

## Nathan "Nearest" Green

Green was hired by Jack Daniel's Distillery to be their first master distiller and is the first African American master distiller on record in the United States. Green was born into slavery and was emancipated after the Civil War. He taught his distilling techniques to Jack Daniel, founder of the eponymous Tennessee whiskey distillery.

In August 2017, Brown-Forman Corporation, which owns the Jack Daniel's Distillery, officially recognized Green as Jack Daniel's first head stiller (now called master distiller) and added him to the company's website.

## Evan Williams

Evan Williams was a Welsh immigrant who became a Louisville councilman and the city's first harbormaster. In 1783, he is reported to have founded Kentucky's first commercial distillery on the banks of the Ohio River. There is some debate as to the truth of this, since records in those days were poorly kept, but there is no doubt that Williams was an outspoken leader, entrepreneur, and key figure in the rise of bourbon.

## Basil Hayden

Meredith Basil Hayden Sr. holds the distinction of having two bourbons named after him. A descendant of a wealthy Catholic family from England, he led a group of families from Maryland into what is now Nelson County, Kentucky, in 1785 and donated the land to build the first Catholic church in the commonwealth. In 1885, his grandson Raymond B. Hayden founded a distillery in Nelson County and named it Old Grand-Dad after his grandfather. The Old Grand-Dad label still bears Basil Hayden's portrait. In 1992, Jim Beam introduced a small-batch bourbon named Basil Hayden's, using a mash bill similar to the one used by its namesake in the 1780s.

## J. W. Dant

Joseph Washington Dant was born in 1820 on a farm in Loretto, Kentucky. He was a blacksmith who opened his own distillery in 1836 at the age of sixteen. He became famous for being the first commercial distillery to utilize the log still method, in which a hollowed-out tree trunk and copper piping are used to make the distillate for bourbon. While modern J. W. Dant bourbon is not made in this manner, Dant's spirit of ingenuity lives on.

## John E. Fitzgerald

The lore and lineage of John E. Fitzgerald is a convoluted tale that links some of Kentucky's finest bourbon makers together. The story is told in many a book, including Sally Van Winkle Campbell's *But Always Fine Bourbon*. Essentially, John Fitzgerald was a larger-than-life distiller who had a taste for the finest bourbons in the world. The Stitzel-Weller Distillery produced a brand honoring John E., naming it Old Fitzgerald. It was eventually sold to Julian P. ("Pappy") Van Winkle Sr. and became one of the first great wheated bourbons. Stitzel-Weller, in addition to Old Fitzgerald, also produced brands such as W. L. Weller, Pappy Van Winkle, and Rebel Yell, among others. These brands have passed through numerous hands and are produced at various distilleries today, but all have their roots in John E. Fitzgerald, one of the grand forefathers of modern bourbon.

## Jim Beam

Colonel James Beauregard Beam was born in 1864 at the tail end of the Civil War. Before Prohibition, he ran what was then called the Old Tub Distillery, which he inherited from his father. When Prohibition ended, Beam bought the Murphy, Barber & Co. Distillery and made whiskey under the "Colonel James B. Beam" label. In the 1950s, his son T. Jeremiah Beam launched the Jim Beam brand to honor his father. It has since become one of the most recognizable bourbon labels in the world.

# THE CHEF

# LAWRENCE WEEKS

There's a historical bourbon connection between Louisville and New Orleans that happens via the Ohio and Mississippi Rivers. Once you taste the Cajun/Creole cuisine of Lawrence Weeks, you come to understand that there's a culinary connection as well. Lawrence grew up in Louisville but has traveled and cooked throughout the American South, working under some of the best names in Southern food. It's his time to shine, and he does so brilliantly at North of Bourbon in Louisville, where his exploration of Louisiana food is told through a Louisville lens.

**Q:** *What's the best thing to eat with a neat pour of bourbon?*

**A:** I usually keep this a secret, so this is some insider trade information, but my favorite pairing is actually a neat pour and a few slices of Braunschweiger [sausage] with whatever you'd like with it: crackers, mustard, pickles. I think the sweetness and smoke of the bourbon go perfectly with that style of charcuterie.

**Q:** *Your restaurant has "bourbon" in the name. How much did you consider the flavors of bourbon when coming up with the menu?*

**A:** For our restaurant concept, bourbon was more in consideration with the cocktail program and the three hundred–plus pours of bourbon we offer. I generally cook food that I consider pairs nicely with bourbon rather than putting it in many of our dishes.

**Q:** *What do you like about cooking with bourbon?*

**A:** I personally enjoy that bourbon can be added at various stages of cooking and it sings a different note depending on when it's added: sweetness when it's cooked down, spice and sharpness when it's added "raw."

**Q:** *There's a definite bourbon connection between Kentucky and New Orleans. Is there a food connection as well?*

**A:** The connection between Kentucky and NOLA definitely comes in the influence of trade routes on the river. That translates to a multicultural mix of French, German, Irish, African American, etc. You'll see much of the same dishes in New Orleans, minus the same preservation traditions. The weather conditions down there don't do much justice to fermentation pickling.

**Q:** *You grew up in Louisville. Was the culture of bourbon something you grew up with? How old were you when you first tasted bourbon?*

**A:** I grew up with bourbon being the significant spirit in the house. Being that my father is Lexington-born and New York City–raised, I'm sure after his stint away from Kentucky it was a warm welcome back home. As a young'un, I remember smelling a bourbon and Coke and thinking the vanilla and sweetness smelled so good. I can't tell you the first time I tried bourbon, but I'm certain it would be self-incriminating, so I plead the Fifth . . . but I drank it, too.

# THE PROPER WAY
# TO TASTE BOURBON

"Too much of anything is bad, but too much good whiskey is barely enough."

—ATTRIBUTED TO MARK TWAIN

The simple answer is, there is no proper way—smell and taste bourbon however you like, and don't let others determine your enjoyment of your bourbon. However, there are a few rules that can guide you to a more enjoyable experience if you want to dive into a proper tasting. Whiskey is not wine, so a lot of the methods used in wine tasting don't apply here. You can't hold your nose right up to the bourbon, as the alcohol will burn your nostrils. Remember, bourbon can be anywhere from 80 to 100 proof or more, and inhaling a whiff of that will only make you choke. I like to keep my nose a good 6 to 8 inches away from the edge of the glass while giving it a swirl. You want to waft the aroma into your nostrils.

Another great way to smell bourbon is to pour a small amount of the bourbon into a glass, like a Glencairn glass (see page 50). Swish it around several times and then dump out the bourbon. Now bring your nose right to the glass and cup your other hand around the glass and your face. Now you can inhale deeply and really get a good scent from the residual bourbon in the glass. Close your eyes and try to identify those notes: butterscotch, tobacco, perhaps a little cinnamon, maybe dried figs? It's a fun exercise, and the more you try it, the more you'll find yourself identifying aromas.

Now for the taste. Take a small sip, roll it around in your mouth, and swallow. I usually do this to temper my mouth. If it's my first taste of bourbon of the day, the initial sip is usually a shock to my mouth, and all I get is astringency. It's the

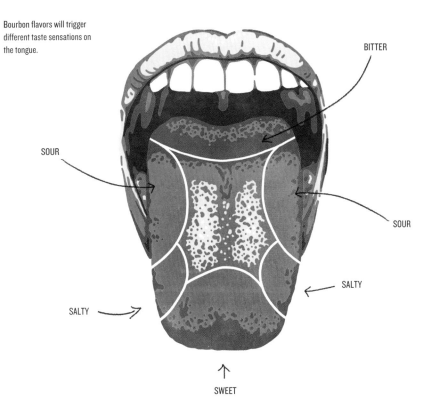

Bourbon flavors will trigger different taste sensations on the tongue.

BITTER

SOUR

SOUR

SALTY

SALTY

SWEET

second sip that counts. Swish it around in your mouth, swallow it slowly, and then smack your lips while lightly exhaling. (This is called the Kentucky Chew.)

Sometimes, it takes several rinses of bourbon in your mouth to feel the Kentucky Hug, the sensations you experience within your mouth, or the mouthfeel of the bourbon. You might find the sides of your tongue prickling with a pleasant burn. You might feel the tip of your tongue reacting to the sugars in the bourbon. You might feel your tongue drying out from its astringency. You might identify a long finish of leather aromas long after the sip has been swallowed. It's a fun exercise to write down these sensations and identify how different bourbons feel on your tongue.

One last thing to remember is that bourbon is high in alcohol. Most of us don't have the stamina to taste through more than a few bourbons before our palate is shot and we're tipsy—at that point, you can put your pen down and just enjoy the bourbon without the nerdy note-taking.

# WHAT IS MOONSHINE, AND IS IT RELATED TO BOURBON?

Moonshine is made all over the South in illegal backyard stills and garages. It can be described as "unaged (and traditionally untaxed) whiskey." Because it is an unregulated product, it can be distilled from anything, from fruit to sugarcane to potatoes. A market for underground whiskey grew during the American Revolution when the newly established United States government placed a tax on spirits to pay for the war. The immigrant whiskey makers from Ireland and England, who had left Europe in part to escape government overstepping, bristled at the idea of this new tax, and some turned to making whiskey in hidden stills deep in the wilderness.

Moonshining was a steady but minor presence in the whiskey world, mostly made up of unorganized backyard bandits trying to evade the law. Prohibition changed that overnight. Moonshine making exploded to supply both speakeasies and individual consumers. Made in secret and transported to big-city speakeasies in souped-up cars to outrun the local sheriffs, this contraband alcohol was often transported during the quiet hours of the night when the moon was out. Sometimes the producers would cut corners, using sugar instead of grain as the base for their spirit, for example, to make a profit. During this period, there were also reports of bootleggers using lead-contaminated car radiators as condensers to distill alcohol, leading to a few instances of lead poisoning. Additionally, some distillers were careless, or outright unscrupulous, and sold hooch that contained or had been cut with methanol (also known as wood alcohol), which can damage the optic nerve or even cause death, depending on how much is consumed. (This is where those tales of people going blind from moonshine originated.)

Tax collectors and sheriffs at the courthouse in Catlettsburg, Kentucky, with confiscated moonshine stills from a 1928 raid.

Once Prohibition was repealed and legal whiskey was readily available on the market, there was a sharp decline in the popularity of moonshine. Yet there were—and still are—moonshiners who wanted to sell their product without being taxed. Unlike bourbon, moonshine doesn't have any federal regulations in place governing what it has to contain or how it has to be produced; this can lead to wildly different products depending on where one purchases it.

Today, the story of moonshine lives on in an array of imaginative products sold legally. Clear distillate in flavors ranging from apple pie to peach tea can be found on the shelves of liquor stores, sometimes bottled in mason jars to make the "moonshine" look homemade. One could argue that the second this distillate is no longer contraband, it ceases to be moonshine, but you can fight that one out with your buddies. The truth is, there's still a small but thriving moonshine culture alive and well in the hinterlands of Kentucky, Tennessee, and beyond. It may be difficult to find, but the good stuff is worth seeking out. I once drank a jar of sorghum moonshine that was so good, I kept telling people we should rename it sunshine because of the way it made me feel!

# LOUISVILLE CITY LIMITS

When you think of bourbon distilleries, you most likely envision vast rolling hills of weather-beaten rickhouses, farmhouse tasting rooms, and country roads with a lush green forest backdrop. This is true of most distilleries in the countryside of Kentucky, but with the rise in popularity of bourbon tourism, you are seeing more and more urban distilleries popping up right in the heart of downtown Louisville. In fact, most of the distilleries in this tour are within walking distance from east to west in downtown Louisville.

Start your day at **COPPER & KINGS** distillery in the Butchertown neighborhood of Louisville. Though they do not actually distill bourbon, much of their gin and brandy is aged in used bourbon barrels, which gives their spirits a bourbon-tinged flavor. They represent the best of a trend that utilizes bourbon barrels to create an entire category of bourbon-finished products that includes beer, gin, syrups, and even soy sauce (see page 142).

Walk through the trendy NuLu neighborhood of Louisville to find one of the more cutting-edge bourbons in **RABBIT HOLE DISTILLERY**—a thoroughly modern facility with sleek architectural edges and one of the city's best hidden rooftop bars. The scent of aged bourbon always reminds me of soft cured leather, so an obvious stop on this tour is Clayton & Crume, who make all the leather goods you don't need but desperately want, including the coolest leather-wrapped glass

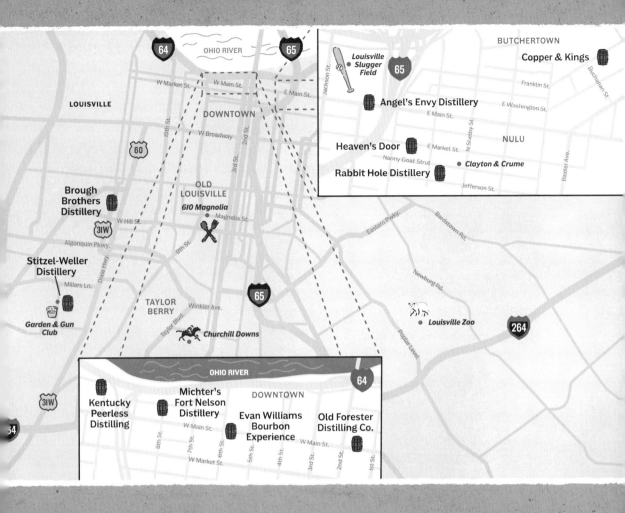

bottle flask for taking your prized bourbon on the go. A quick walk will take you to the newest distillery in the hood, **HEAVEN'S DOOR**, named after a song by the legendary poet Bob Dylan, whose art adorns the bottles.

Your next stop will be at **ANGEL'S ENVY DISTILLERY**, another forward-thinking brand that finishes its bourbon in spent port wine barrels. Take a tour or a cocktail class, or smoke a cigar and watch the minor league baseball team hit home runs at Slugger Field

stadium. You don't get much more Louisville than that. From here, you can visit one of the stalwarts of the bourbon tradition inside the newly built **OLD FORESTER DISTILLING CO.** on West Main Street. Though the building is proudly modern and high-tech, the Old Forester Distilling Co. was actually founded in 1870 by George Garvin Brown and has produced one of the most reliably delicious bourbons throughout its history. If you want to sound like a local ordering booze at a Louisville watering hole, just ask the bartender for an Ol' Fo and water. It'll earn you some street cred.

If you're feeling hungry at this point, there are tons of great restaurants in the downtown corridor, but if I'm doing bourbon in the afternoon, I'm always craving fried chicken, and there's no better spot than Indi's. Located next to a gas station and outfitted with bulletproof glass, this place is mostly a take-out joint, but it hits the spot every time—don't forget to order the boiled greens and Indi's homemade hot sauce.

There are two experiences on the downtown walking tour that are not full-blown operations—though they do distill some bourbon—but are well worth the visit. **MICHTER'S FORT NELSON DISTILLERY** is on the corner of a nostalgic building on West Main Street. They have tours, tastings, and one of the best distillery bars in downtown Louisville. A stone's throw away is the **EVAN WILLIAMS BOURBON EXPERIENCE**, a trailblazer in bringing the bourbon experience to life in an urban location. Their tour is an education in how bourbon has evolved from backwoods to city center.

Walk a little farther west and you'll wander into **KENTUCKY PEERLESS DISTILLING**, which is in a nondescript building in a warehouse neighborhood, far from the throngs of tourists. There's nothing flashy or modern or even convenient about this place, but they make damn good bourbon and rye that sell out faster than they can produce them.

A few other notable spots are farther than walking distance but worth the visit. A quick drive up Dixie Highway will take you to **BROUGH BROTHERS DISTILLERY**, where they produce a wonderful bourbon. As the first Black-owned bourbon distillery in the state, Brough Brothers is also a sign of the promising future of diversity in the bourbon universe.

After all this tasting, I'm usually ready for a well-crafted cocktail. Head over to the Garden & Gun Club at **STITZEL-WELLER DISTILLERY** in Shively for a Southern snack and a stiff cocktail. Stitzel-Weller has a storied history, and you'll learn all about it on their tour. Though it has changed hands several times, the distillery is still making great bourbon, and it's important to have this legendary place alive and well.

It's been a long day, and at this point you have two choices: Get take-out pizza and crash, or keep going for the full Louisville culinary experience. From Stitzel-Weller, you're not far from my flagship restaurant, 610 Magnolia, which offers a tasting menu designed to bring you the best of Kentucky on a plate. And if I'm around, I'll greet you with a hug.

# DISTILLERY CATS

In 2014, one of Woodford Reserve's most beloved employees passed away. His name was Elijah—after Elijah Pepper, the original distiller on the property in 1812—and he was a twenty-year-old orange tabby cat. The former stray had wandered onto the distillery grounds in 1996 and quickly fell into the role of distillery cat-bassador.

After his death, the Twitter hashtag #RememberElijah started to go viral in Kentucky. Elijah wasn't just a pet—he was a big part of the distillery experience, for both staff and guests. Amid the outpouring of love, many commenters shared stories about *other* distillery cats, who have historically held an important (if under-the-radar) position in the state's bourbon industry.

Whenever you have to store any sort of agricultural product, you will, of course, end up with pests. Distillery cats are "employed" to help control the mouse population—think of them like barn cats for whiskey—and in Scotland, distillers still refer to them as mousers. But aside from guarding the grain—something that became less important as distilleries industrialized—many distillery cats become more mascot than mouser.

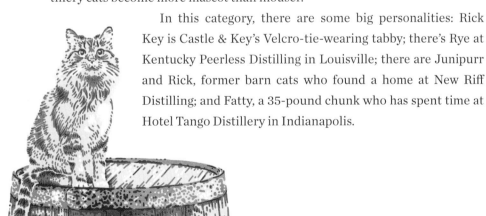

In this category, there are some big personalities: Rick Key is Castle & Key's Velcro-tie-wearing tabby; there's Rye at Kentucky Peerless Distilling in Louisville; there are Junipurr and Rick, former barn cats who found a home at New Riff Distilling; and Fatty, a 35-pound chunk who has spent time at Hotel Tango Distillery in Indianapolis.

# WARM GOAT CHEESE DIP WITH BOURBON-SOAKED CHERRIES

Who doesn't love a good dip? Sharp goat cheese is mellowed by baking until the surface is bubbling and lightly charred. It then gets smothered with cherries dripping in bourbon. Tart, sweet, and smoky, this dip is a great first course that's screaming to be paired with a Gold Rush (page 187).

**Serves 4 to 6**

**FOR THE DIP**

8 ounces goat cheese

2 ounces sour cream

1½ teaspoons bourbon

Kosher salt and freshly ground
    black pepper

**FOR THE BOURBON-SOAKED CHERRIES**

½ tablespoon unsalted butter

I cup dried cherries

¾ cup bourbon

1½ tablespoons sugar

1½ teaspoons balsamic vinegar

½ teaspoon fresh thyme

Crackers, cheese straws, sliced apples, radishes, and sliced toasted sourdough bread, for serving (optional)

Preheat the oven to 385°F.

To make the dip, in a medium bowl, combine the goat cheese, sour cream, bourbon, and salt and pepper to taste. Mix thoroughly. Transfer to an ovenproof shallow dish and bake for 18 minutes. Turn the oven to broil and cook for 2 minutes, or until the top of the dip is lightly browned.

While the goat cheese dip is baking, make the bourbon-soaked cherries: In a small pot, warm the butter over medium-low heat until it foams. Add the dried cherries and gently cook for 1 minute. Add the bourbon, sugar, and vinegar. Cook until the bourbon has reduced and the mixture is syrupy, about 8 minutes. Add the thyme and keep warm until the goat cheese is ready to serve.

When the goat cheese dip comes out of the oven, pour the bourbon-soaked cherries over the top and serve with an assortment of crackers, cheese straws, sliced apples, and toasted sourdough bread slices.

# CORN, AVOCADO, AND PEACH SALAD WITH BOURBON-SESAME VINAIGRETTE

When cooking with bourbon, you can take the flavor in many different directions. You can use older bourbons to focus on the sweeter, richer notes that pair with charred flavors. Or you can highlight the lighter hay, fermented corn, and vegetal notes more prevalent in young bourbons (less than five years of age). They play beautifully with fresh summer ingredients that are bursting with natural sugars. This summer salad is bright and succulent, held together by the light, creamy dressing redolent of young bourbon.

### Serves 2

1½ cups vegetable oil

¾ cup cooked chickpeas, drained

Kosher salt and freshly ground
    black pepper

2 ears corn, shucked

2 peaches, pitted and sliced

I avocado, pitted and sliced

½ cup fresh Thai basil leaves, torn

2 cups arugula

Bourbon-Sesame Vinaigrette
    (recipe follows)

In a small pot, heat the oil until it reaches 325°F on an instant-read thermometer. Add the chickpeas and cook for 6 minutes, until golden and crispy. Remove with a slotted spoon and drain on a paper towel–lined plate. Season with salt and pepper.

Using a sharp knife, cut the corn kernels off the cob and place them in a large bowl. Add the peach and avocado slices to the bowl, then add the basil and arugula and toss. Add 1¼ cups of the vinaigrette, season with salt and pepper, and gently toss.

Divide the salad between two plates, top with the crispy chickpeas, and drizzle a little more vinaigrette over the top. Serve immediately.

« CONTINUED »

# BOURBON-SESAME VINAIGRETTE

The creaminess of the tahini brings out the sweetness in the bourbon in this velvety dressing that proves how versatile bourbon can be.

**Makes ¾ cup**

½ cup bourbon

¼ cup tahini

3 tablespoons fresh lemon juice, plus more if needed

2 tablespoons olive oil

1 teaspoon honey

Kosher salt and freshly ground black pepper

In a small pot, bring the bourbon to a simmer over high heat and cook until reduced to 3 tablespoons, 3 to 4 minutes. Transfer the reduced bourbon to a small bowl and add the tahini, lemon juice, olive oil, and honey. Whisk well to combine. Taste for seasoning, adding salt, pepper, and more lemon juice as needed. Store in an airtight container in the fridge for up to 3 weeks. Whisk again before using.

# CHILLED CORN AND BOURBON SOUP

Bourbon is made from fermented dried corn. Corn is at its peak in summer, when a chilled soup is the best thing to cool down a swampy July evening. This dish links the origin flavor of corn to the aged flavors in bourbon and proves how beautifully they pair with each other.

**Serves 4 as an appetizer**

4 ears corn, shucked

4 cups vegetable stock

2 tablespoons unsalted butter

¼ cup chopped onion

I garlic clove, peeled

I cup bourbon

¼ cup buttermilk

¼ cup heavy cream

Kosher salt and freshly ground black pepper

Olive oil

I scallion, finely chopped, for garnish

Turn a gas burner to high. Holding the corn with tongs, toast it over the flame for 2 minutes, or until there are char marks on the kernels. (Alternatively, preheat the oven to 500°F. Place the corn on a rack and cook for 8 minutes until toasted.) Let it cool for a few minutes, then cut the kernels from the cobs and place them in a bowl, reserving 2 of the cobs. Set aside until ready to simmer.

Place the reserved corncobs in a pot with the stock. Simmer for 15 minutes, then strain the liquid. Discard the corncobs.

In a separate pot, melt the butter over medium heat. When it foams, add the onion and garlic and cook for 3 minutes, until wilted. Deglaze the pan with the bourbon, scraping the bottom of the pan with a spatula, and simmer for 5 minutes, until the bourbon has reduced. Add the corn kernels and cook for 5 minutes, then add the corn stock and simmer for 20 minutes.

**« CONTINUED »**

Add the buttermilk and cream and simmer for 5 minutes more. Remove from the heat and let the soup cool to room temperature.

Puree the soup in a blender on high, or blend it directly in the pot using an immersion blender. Strain the pureed soup through a sieve, discarding the solids. Season with salt and pepper, then refrigerate the soup, uncovered, until chilled, at least 3 hours.

Pour the chilled soup into bowls and garnish with a drizzle of olive oil, fresh cracked pepper, and chopped scallion before serving.

# WATERMELON, MINT, FETA, AND FRIED PEANUT SALAD

In Louisville, we drink mint juleps once a year during the Kentucky Derby. I'm not a big fan of the cocktail, but I do love the pairing of bourbon and mint, which works great in a salad. Add some watermelon for sweetness, feta for saltiness, and fried peanuts to tie everything together with a crunchy nuttiness. Serve this salad as a side or a first course.

**Serves 8 as a side**

8 cups cubed watermelon

I cup fresh mint, chopped

3 ounces feta cheese, crumbled

2 tablespoons sesame seeds

I tablespoon olive oil

I teaspoon fresh lemon juice

I cup unsalted peanuts

I½ teaspoons sugar

I tablespoon bourbon

2 teaspoons soy sauce

¼ teaspoon Bourbon Salt (page 78)

Place the watermelon cubes in a large bowl. Add the mint, feta, sesame seeds, olive oil, and lemon juice. Toss gently until just combined.

In a sauté pan, roast the peanuts over medium heat until just lightly toasted, about 2 minutes. Add the sugar, bourbon, and soy sauce. Shake the pan vigorously to combine all the ingredients. The liquid will cook off quickly; when the pan is almost dry, transfer the peanuts to a plate and let cool to room temperature.

Plate the watermelon salad in individual bowls and top with the peanuts. Sprinkle a little bourbon salt over the top. Serve right away.

# BOURBON-CURED SALMON SALAD

Alcohol is an effective way to cure fish. Here the bourbon cuts through the fattiness of the salmon while adding a layer of smoky flavor. It's a subtle taste, but not everything bourbon has to be a tattooed arm wrestler hurling food at you like a sledgehammer. Bourbon can be soft, elegant, and nuanced. It can be a barely noticeable flavor and still contribute much to a dish.

This recipe, like any house-cured fish, will take a few days to prepare, so plan accordingly.

**Serves 4**

### FOR THE SALMON

I pound salmon fillet,
    skin removed (see Note)

½ cup kosher salt

¼ cup sugar

2 tablespoons bourbon

I tablespoon ground coffee

I teaspoon freshly ground
    black pepper

### FOR THE SALAD

I bunch dandelion greens

4 radishes, thinly sliced

2 endives, leaves separated

8 fresh lychees, peeled, pitted,
    and halved

Bourbon Vinaigrette (recipe follows)

Kosher salt and freshly ground
    black pepper

To prepare the salmon, when you bring it home, remove it from the wrapper as soon as you can and pat dry with paper towels.

In a medium bowl, mix together the salt, sugar, bourbon, coffee, and pepper until evenly combined.

Place a ceramic or glass baking dish that fits the salmon on your work surface. Scatter half the salt mixture over the bottom of the dish. Place the salmon on top. Spread the remaining salt mixture over the top of the salmon. Cover with plastic wrap, pressing it right against the top of the fish. Weigh it down with something heavy, like another baking dish or a stack of small plates. Refrigerate for 3 days.

**« CONTINUED »**

After day 3, remove the salmon and scrape off the salt mixture. Give the fish a rinse under cold running water for 1 minute. Line a clean plate with several layers of paper towels. Place the salmon on the plate and refrigerate, uncovered, for 24 hours.

The next day, when you are ready to make the salad, slice 24 thin slices of the cured salmon. Store any remaining salmon in an airtight container in the fridge for up to 3 days.

To make the salad, in a large bowl, combine the dandelion greens, radishes, endives, and lychees. Drizzle with a little vinaigrette. Season with salt and pepper.

Arrange the salad on four plates. Top each with 6 slices of the bourbon-cured salmon and spoon a little more vinaigrette over everything. Serve immediately.

**NOTE:** Get a thicker fillet, if possible, closer to the head of the fish for even curing. Ask your fishmonger to remove the pinbones.

## BOURBON VINAIGRETTE

This is a favorite dressing that I use in virtually every salad I make at home. It's a classic vinaigrette with a distinctive whiskey aroma, and it will work nicely with any cold or raw vegetable preparation.

**Makes 1 cup**

¼ cup bourbon

¾ cup olive oil

2 tablespoons apple cider vinegar

1 tablespoon pure maple syrup

½ teaspoon freshly ground black pepper

¼ teaspoon kosher salt

In a small saucepan, bring the bourbon to a boil over medium heat. Cook until the bourbon has reduced to 2 tablespoons, 3 to 4 minutes. Transfer to a small bowl. Add the olive oil, vinegar, maple syrup, pepper, and salt and whisk until combined. Store in a lidded jar in the fridge for up to 7 days. Whisk again before using.

# CORN DOG WITH BOURBON MUSTARD

Here's a solid, time-honored recipe for a classic fairground favorite paired with a bourbon-spiked mustard. I've heard that some people eat corn dogs with ketchup, too, but to me, that's just adding another sauce to an already perfect dish.

**Serves 4**

2 quarts corn oil, for frying

4 hot dogs

1¼ cups buttermilk

I large egg

I cup cornmeal

I cup all-purpose flour

3 tablespoons sugar

2 tablespoons unsalted butter, melted

I tablespoon baking powder

½ teaspoon kosher salt

Bourbon Mustard (recipe follows), for serving

SPECIAL EQUIPMENT

2 pairs disposable wooden or bamboo chopsticks

In a heavy pot, heat the corn oil over high heat until it reaches 375°F on an instant-read thermometer.

Separate the chopsticks and use one to skewer each hot dog, inserting the chopstick at least halfway.

In a large bowl, mix together the buttermilk, egg, cornmeal, flour, sugar, melted butter, baking powder, and salt until combined. Let rest for 10 minutes.

Dip each hot dog in the batter, shake off any excess, and deep-fry in the hot oil until the surface is puffed up and golden brown, 3 to 4 minutes. Remove the corn dog and let drain on a paper towel–lined plate.

Serve immediately, drizzled with bourbon mustard.

« CONTINUED »

# BOURBON MUSTARD

This is a version of honey mustard amped up with a shot of bourbon. It's a simple way to smooth the sharpness of yellow mustard.

**Makes ¼ cup**

½ cup bourbon, reduced to
   2 tablespoons (see page 75)
¼ cup yellow mustard

I teaspoon honey
Dash of Worcestershire sauce
Pinch of freshly ground black pepper

In a small bowl, whisk together the reduced bourbon, mustard, honey, Worcestershire, and pepper. Use immediately or store in the fridge in a lidded container for up to 2 weeks.

# ROASTED SWEET POTATO WITH BOURBON-MISO BUTTER

When I think about pairing bourbon with vegetables, I want a veg that can stand toe to toe with the sweetness of bourbon but with an earthy component and a texture that can capture the melty drip of bourbon. The answer is easy—the mighty roasted sweet potato.

**Serves 2 as a side**

2 sweet potatoes

2 teaspoons olive oil

I tablespoon coarse salt

½ cup corn oil

2 sprigs rosemary

½ cup Bourbon-Miso Butter
  (recipe follows)

¼ teaspoon red pepper flakes

Preheat the oven to 400°F.

Rub the sweet potatoes with the olive oil and sprinkle all over with the salt. Place each sweet potato on a large square of aluminum foil and wrap tightly. Place the sweet potatoes on a sheet pan and bake for about 45 minutes, until the flesh is soft to the touch. Remove the sheet pan from the oven but wait 5 minutes before unwrapping the sweet potatoes.

Meanwhile, in a small pot, heat the corn oil over high heat until it reaches 375°F on an instant-read thermometer. Remove the rosemary needles from the stems. Add the rosemary to the hot oil and fry for 40 seconds, until crispy. Immediately use a spider to skim out the rosemary and drain on a paper towel.

Place the hot sweet potatoes on a plate or cutting board. Using a sharp paring knife, make a slit in the top all the way down the length of the sweet potato. Push the bottom of the sweet potato on opposite sides with both hands to open up the flesh. Top with a dollop of the bourbon-miso butter. Garnish with the fried rosemary and a few sprinkles of red pepper flakes. Serve right away, while the sweet potato is still hot and the butter hasn't completely melted.

# BOURBON-MISO BUTTER

This butter was made to coat the flesh of a roasted sweet potato, but it melts equally deliciously on everything from roasted leeks to steamed clams. Experiment to see what other delicacies you can pair with it. The butter will keep for up to 4 weeks in your fridge, so feel free to make extra.

**Makes 1½ cups**

6 tablespoons bourbon

2 tablespoons dark miso paste

2 tablespoons light brown sugar

1½ teaspoons toasted sesame oil

2 garlic cloves, minced

Zest of 1 lemon

1 cup (2 sticks) unsalted butter, at room temperature

In a small pot, simmer the bourbon over medium heat until reduced by half. Add the miso, brown sugar, sesame oil, garlic, and lemon zest. Bring back to a simmer. Transfer the mixture to a small bowl and let cool until just slightly warm to the touch.

Place the butter in a large bowl. Drizzle in the warm bourbon mixture a little at a time and whisk to combine with the butter. When all the liquid has been incorporated, transfer the compound butter to a lidded container or roll it into 1½-inch-thick logs and wrap in plastic wrap. Chill the butter in the fridge for at least 1 hour before using. Make sure to bring the butter back to room temperature before serving. Store in the fridge for up to 4 weeks.

# BOURBON COFFEE–GLAZED HAM STEAK WITH FRIED APPLES

It might be a poor decision to have bourbon for breakfast, but you can apply a bourbon-coffee glaze to ham and eat it morning or night. This is a breakfast that will wake up your taste buds. Serve it with a fried egg for a complete meal.

**Serves 2**

3 teaspoons pork fat or unsalted butter

¾ pound ham steak

1 apple, peeled, cored, and cut into 8 wedges

2 tablespoons honey

1 tablespoon bourbon

2 teaspoons brewed coffee

1 teaspoon apple cider vinegar

2 large eggs

Kosher salt and freshly ground black pepper

In a large cast-iron skillet, melt 1½ teaspoons of the pork fat over medium-high heat. Add the ham steak and apples and cook for 5 minutes, until both are lightly browned. Transfer the apples to a plate; leave the ham in the pan.

Meanwhile, in a small bowl, stir together the honey, bourbon, coffee, and vinegar. Add this glaze to the pan with the ham. Cook for 3 to 4 minutes to reduce the glaze. Flip the ham steak and cook for 2 minutes more, or until the glaze sticks to the ham.

In a separate small pan, melt the remaining 1½ teaspoons pork fat. Crack the eggs into the pan and cook them sunny-side up, about 2 minutes. Season with salt and pepper.

Cut the ham in half and transfer the ham steaks to two plates. Place a fried egg on top of each ham steak. Divide the fried apples between the plates. Scoop up any glaze left in the pan and drizzle it over the top. Season with salt and pepper and serve immediately.

# OAK AND SPICE

Bourbon carries an age statement, which tells you how long the bourbon has aged in an oak barrel. That could be as few as four years; it could be as many as twenty years. That's a long time to wait for a sip of bourbon. But older still is the age of the white oak tree that gave itself to the making of the barrel in which the bourbon aged.

Oak trees do not grow fast. They are not shade-intolerant. They climb to the heavens in a steady pace, straight and strong. Some trees can be harvested in fifty years, others will take seventy to eighty years to mature. That's an entire lifetime. When you swirl a glass of bourbon under your nose and inhale the vanilla and spice aromas lent to the liquid by the oak barrel, you're smelling decades of sunlight and soil and rain and patience.

In Gravel Switch, Kentucky, there's an oak tree farm owned by the Taylor family. One day, Scott Taylor drives me through the property on his ATV. He's the son of Clifton and Barbara Taylor, whose family have been caretakers of this unforgiving land since the late 1700s. Scott is a Kentucky master logger and the father of Josh Taylor, who has just had an infant daughter. Generations are important in this family, because this industry is one that demands patience. At my restaurant, I churn out food nightly; it is instant gratification. The farmers I work with see the world through the lens of months. Bourbon folks think in terms of decades. But a family that raises and sells oak trees thinks in terms of generations.

I have to hang on tightly with both hands as the ATV groans up muddy hills and whips through creeks. Branches slap me in the face. Scott tells me to be wary of turkey mites and spiders the size of my fist. Theirs is not a farm in the traditional sense. There are no tracts of land with trees planted in rows. It is a wild habitat. There are also poplar and walnut and red oak trees growing. Deer and turtles and songbirds live on the land. To the untrained eye, it's just a wild forest. But there is a delicate control—what Chris Will calls regenerative farming.

Chris Will is a consulting forester. He's a one-man show on a mission to train tree farmers how to responsibly regenerate white oak forests. He's worked in timber and sawmills and at universities. He's worked with the Taylor family for years, consulting on their tree farm. The way they explain their process seems simple, yet a lot goes into it. "We manage our white oak so that we only cut a tree when we know we have another tree growing to replace it; we manage wilderness," Chris tells me.

Trees compete for light. The forest is a brutal competition for survival. Red maples, for example, will grow under a canopy because they are shade-tolerant. The young white oak will not. Much of Scott's work is managing canopy. A dense maple canopy will drown out any chance of a white oak seedling's survival. Under the dense canopy in the middle of the day, there isn't a drop of sunlight seeping through the overstory. The soil is wet. There are fossils of mollusks and aquatic creatures from the Cretaceous to be found along the creek beds. The air is cool and moist. Scott talks a lot about wildlife, which may sound odd for a tree farmer. He points out a locust tree where an owl has made a nest for its young. He identifies the tracks of a wolf pack that roams through the forest at night. It's important to Scott that this forest is a safe haven for wildlife. I soon realize that this livelihood is not strictly commerce for the Taylor family. They care deeply about the land. Life in the woodlands was hard generations ago. There were no hospitals, no schools. Danger lurked around every tree. Back then, the average human life span was about thirty-five. Even today, Scott warns me about heavy falling branches that can kill you instantly.

What I see at the white oak stands is unreal. Giant tree trunks extending straight up to the sky. Spaced about 25 feet apart, forty to sixty trees per acre. The sunlight is dappled. The soil is dry, and the southern exposure provides plenty of sunlight. Scott explains what makes a good oak tree: tall, straight, and limb-free, with no knots. The goal is a moderate crown, 30 to 40 percent of the volume of that tree. An ideal diameter for a white oak is 17 to 27 inches. Bourbon barrels are made only with wood from the lower portion of the tree, where there aren't too many limbs. The rest of the tree gets sold as timber. I ask Scott what pays better, the bourbon industry or the timber industry.

"Timber prices are so high, we can sell all these trees and cash out big, but that's not what we want," says Scott. They did that back after the Civil War and ruined the land. "Most regeneration is not from acorns but from root sprout, so you have to let a tree mature enough to do a root sprout before you cut down the tree. And oaks won't sprout until about twenty years old." He points up at the treetops. "Look at that crown—it has spots and holes, which provides this filtered light, which is the right window for oak seedlings to build strong roots."

One of bourbon's looming problems is how to supply enough barrels. The rise in bourbon's popularity has created staggering demand for barrels, which means demand for white oak trees. By law, charred oak barrels can be used only once in bourbon production. But trees don't care about our escalating consumption of bourbon. They take their time to grow. Efforts are underway, like the White Oak Initiative, to raise awareness and bring the smartest minds together to solve this issue, but there's no clear answer.

The problem is that only specific white oak trees can be used for bourbon barrels, and they grow in the region of the Midwest from the Ozarks to Appalachia, from Illinois to Tennessee, where the climate is ideal for white oaks. Anything too far north, and the resulting wood is too brittle; too far south, and the wood is too porous. Cooperages have experimented with other trees—birch, hickory, poplar—but they don't work. White oak has the perfect trinity of density, sturdiness, and flavor. The wood contains cellular structures known as tyloses that make it watertight so the barrels will not leak. The Romans knew this, which is why they built their ships out of oak.

At a clearing in the forest, the Taylors are planning a new home for white oaks. Nothing growing in the clearing is higher than my knee. Chris Will is passionate about something we can't envision yet. "We can't wait till the crisis. The forest inventory is in trouble; we are not regenerating well enough. White oak's reproductive strategy requires mycelium and soil development and high nutrients. These trees are adapted to this region. The climate here is good, the amount of rainfall, how the soil has developed geologically. The four seasons are important. There is a microbial system that is in harmony here."

I come across an oak sapling barely 3 feet high. It is vulnerable and exposed, basically just a shoot I could tear out with my bare hands. Its chances of becoming a mature oak without the help of these farmers is very small. I understand this forest as a competitive fight for survival. Scott Taylor bends down to touch the sapling and says, "My granddaughter will cut down this tree."

# THE FLAVORS IN WHITE OAK

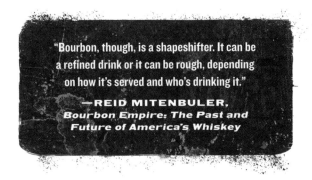

"Bourbon, though, is a shapeshifter. It can be a refined drink or it can be rough, depending on how it's served and who's drinking it."

—REID MITENBULER,
*Bourbon Empire: The Past and Future of America's Whiskey*

Charred white oak gives bourbon its distinctive flavor. It possesses compounds called lignans that break down and turn into vanillin, which gives bourbon its irresistible quality. Vanillin, as the name suggests, is akin to the flavors in vanilla, but additional flavors get coaxed out of the wood, like caramel, butterscotch, and toasted coconut. Some experts claim that charred white oak tastes like crème brûlée. Other chemicals like eugenol and wood lignans get released over time and contribute to flavor as well. Furfural is another important chemical that results from the caramelizing cellulose during the toasting or burning process of the white oak wood. This results in flavors that are typically described as butterscotch, caramel, and toasted almond. Bourbon, despite popular belief, is not a sweet drink. There's no actual sugar in bourbon. But it possesses notes like vanilla and caramel and dried fruit that are perceived as sweet by the person drinking it. These flavors all exist within white oak, which is why it is the preferred wood for aging bourbon.

# STRAIGHT BOURBON VS. BLENDED BOURBON

"Straight bourbon" simply means the bourbon in the bottle has been aged for at least two years in new charred oak barrels. Straight bourbon can carry an age statement on the bottle, but that age statement must reflect the *youngest* bourbon in the bottle. Straight bourbon by law cannot contain any added colorings or flavorings. This designation may seem somewhat obvious in an age when most of the market is dominated by quality bourbon, but this was not the case in the early days of bourbon making, when many additives were stirred into whiskey to mimic the color and flavor of aged bourbon.

"Blended" has often been considered a dirty word in the world of bourbon. Legally, per the Alcohol and Tobacco Tax and Trade Bureau (TTB), a "blended bourbon" has to include only 51 percent straight bourbon, and the mash bill must meet the legal requirements to be called bourbon, namely that it is 51 percent corn.

So what makes up the other 49 percent of the blend? That depends on the distiller, of course. While some companies use this as a loophole to fill the remaining 49 percent of their product with cheap additives or artificial coloring, many American bourbon distilleries have used the allowance to make a genuinely tasty blended product.

This is not to be confused with a category called "blended whiskey," which in the United States must be produced using no less than 20 percent whiskey by volume. The remainder can be grain-neutral spirits. Some of this is based on archaic laws and labeling systems that make little sense in the modern distilling world. There are some purists who insist on drinking only straight bourbons, but many would argue that as the demand for bourbon skyrockets, we will be seeing a steep rise in the number of quality blended bourbons on the market.

# BARRELS AFTER BOURBON

After the aging process takes place, bourbon is drained from the barrel and sent to the bottling plant. What happens to the barrel after that? You might think it has served its purpose and its life span is at an end—but that's far from reality. There is value in spent barrels, and they're used in a variety of ways.

Though the barrel is empty, it is inevitable that, after years of aging, some of the liquid will still saturate the oak staves. There will be a trace amount of spirit clinging to an empty barrel, and the longer the age statement on the bourbon, the stronger the flavor of bourbon in the wood. This has led to the increased utilization of barrel rinsing, a method implemented by Brown-Forman where a used bourbon barrel is filled about halfway with water and allowed to sit for at least three weeks to extract whiskey from the wood fibers.

This proves how much flavor is left in an aged bourbon barrel. With the rise in bourbon's popularity, there has also been a sharp increase in companies taking advantage of "finishing" products in bourbon barrels to infuse some of the bourbon and oak flavors into various liquids.

The most historic and well-documented use for used bourbon barrels is the aging of Scotch whisky. Nine out of ten casks used to mature Scotch were initially used to mature bourbon or Tennessee whiskey. Thousands of empty barrels are shipped to Scotland every year, creating an organic and symbiotic relationship between Scotch and bourbon. In recent years, there's even been a trend of barrel-aging *beer* in used bourbon barrels; these tend to be dark and rich stouts and porters. Greg Hall of Goose Island first popularized this method, and the momentum hasn't let up since.

Here are some other interesting uses for spent bourbon barrels:

- To give their proprietary hot sauce a punch of oak and umami, Tabasco has been aging their chile pepper mash in spent whiskey barrels since the early 1900s. At any given time, their warehouse will have more than seventy thousand barrels of their pepper mash aging in storage.

- Bluegrass Soy Sauce is microbrewed in small batches using only Kentucky-grown non-GMO whole soybeans, soft red winter wheat, and limestone-filtered spring water. The soybean mash is then fermented and aged in repurposed bourbon barrels. The resulting soy sauce is smoky and sweet with a hint of tannin.

- Louisville's Good Folks Coffee partnered with landmark bourbon brand Pappy Van Winkle to create Pappy & Company Bourbon Barrel-Aged Coffee, made with single-origin Guatemalan beans aged in Pappy Van Winkle bourbon barrels.

- Pappy & Company also makes a hot sauce and a maple syrup aged in used bourbon barrels. Both have a unique flavor that is specific to barrel finishing.

- Runamok is a Vermont-based brand that released one of the first bourbon barrel-aged maple syrups. It has been a bestseller since day one.

Barrels are used not only to make edible products but also to provide aesthetic beauty. There's a brisk business in using bourbon staves as an interior design element for walls, bars, chairs, serving trays—basically anything that can be shaped out of a long, thin piece of wood.

Given the rise in demand for used bourbon barrels, the cost of an old bourbon barrel has increased significantly over the years. So much so that it's becoming rare to see a spent bourbon barrel in one of its best and earliest uses: as a table on which you can rest your favorite glass of bourbon.

# CLASSIC OLD-FASHIONED

In 2022, the world lost Marie Zahn, a wonderful human who transformed the cocktail world in Louisville, Kentucky, during her intense but all-too-brief life on earth. This is her recipe for a classic old-fashioned, which is the first drink she ever made for me.

**Makes I**

I½ ounces bourbon

I tablespoon simple syrup

6 drops bitters

I small orange peel, for garnish

Place a large ice cube in a large rocks glass. Add the bourbon, simple syrup, and bitters to the glass. Twist the orange peel and place it in the glass. Enjoy.

"Whiskeys that have been discontinued are like armchair time travel, at least for a moment."
—MARIE ZAHN

# WOMEN AND WHISKEY

Some hold the perception that bourbon is a manly drink, and the films and advertising of the last few decades have surely fortified this narrative. Bourbon is a drink for everyone. Perhaps the rest of the country hasn't caught up with Kentucky yet on this front. According to Fred Minnick, author of *Whiskey Women*, women make up about 37 percent of whiskey drinkers today, compared to 15 percent in the 1990s. Minnick also describes the 1970s and '80s, when bourbon's popularity plummeted across all sectors, as "lost decades" for women in whiskey.

In terms of flavor, there has always been a misperception that somehow smoky, burnt, and bold flavors are masculine and floral notes are feminine— whiskey is for men and wine is for women. I find this narrative to be as inaccurate as it is sexist. And I also find the conventional notion of bourbon being all smoke to be inaccurate. While char and smoke and tobacco are the primary flavors in most bourbons, there are also fruity and floral notes that are secondary but assuredly present. Good bourbon with some age on it has a fruit-leather quality that can range from dark cherry to fig. Many bourbons will have a slightly eucalyptus note, and hints of cinnamon, nutmeg, and allspice. These important taste profiles lurk just behind the sugar and smoke. They are seductive; they are subtle and complex. If that's not feminine, I don't know what is.

# THE DISTILLER

# ELIZABETH McCALL

Woodford Reserve master distiller Elizabeth McCall is the second generation of her family to work in the bourbon industry. McCall has a master's degree from the University of Louisville and has been a member of Brown-Forman's R&D team since 2009. She followed in her mother's footsteps, starting as a sensory expert and working in the quality department. More recently, her role has focused on innovation and the development of new products within the Woodford Reserve brand. She also teaches a class on sensory methodology through bourbon tastings. She has a special way of connecting with people and taking them through that often confusing process of tasting bourbon in a way that's easily relatable.

**Q:** *What's your favorite bourbon cocktail?*

**A:** My favorite bourbon cocktail is a Manhattan, served up in a coupe.

**Q:** *I think you studied psychology in college. Has that helped you in your path to becoming a master distiller?*

**A:** I studied psychology in undergrad and graduate school but started in the beverage alcohol industry before I actually became a therapist. However, I put my therapy skills to use every day in my work as assistant master distiller. Reading a room, consumer trends, presenting, and sensory all require psychology; it touches every part of life.

**Q:** *Is bourbon a masculine drink?*

**A:** Bourbon has long been perceived as "masculine" because it was marketed to white men, and going back before major marketing campaigns, women weren't even allowed in bars or to be seen consuming higher-proof spirits. It wasn't ladylike; wine was what was acceptable. Later, marketing groups focused their advertising on men. It wasn't socially acceptable for women to drink bourbon, and if they did, it was to be in a "dressed-up" cocktail. Today we are starting to change perceptions, but I personally still have a lot of women tell me, "Bourbon is too hot or high proof," and that's why they don't drink it and stick to wine. One thing we do know for sure is that women are driving the growth of the bourbon category. Women typically hold the buying power in their homes and have a growing general interest in drinking a spirit that has flavor and that doesn't need to be mixed.

**Q:** *Do you feel some responsibility for paving the way for more women in the bourbon industry?*

**A:** I feel a level of responsibility to help change what a "master distiller" looks like. We are shining a light on it because women in the bourbon industry are not the norm, we are outliers. I hope that I, and all the other women I work with in the bourbon industry, change the stereotype so we don't have to shine a light on it anymore. That my daughter will grow up believing it's normal for a woman to be a master distiller leading a major brand.

**Q:** *What's the best part of your job?*

**A:** I love when I can turn someone who is not a fan of bourbon into a fan and nerd out with bourbon enthusiasts who ask a million questions. These interactions always remind me of what makes our industry so magical and exciting.

# WHICH CAME FIRST: BOURBON WHISKEY OR BOURBON STREET?

While many assume that New Orleans's Bourbon Street—famous for its many, many bars—was named after the spirit, the timing doesn't quite work to support that theory. The French claimed Louisiana in the 1690s, and after Jean-Baptiste Le Moyne de Bienville founded New Orleans in 1718, a team of royal engineers and architects set about developing the city. They were led by Adrien de Pauger, who designed the city's layout and was responsible for naming its streets.

De Pauger wanted to honor various sectors of French royalty in his naming of the streets but was cognizant that there were simmering power struggles between many members of the country's aristocracy, so as a buffer, he separated some of the streets named for French royalty, like Dumaine and Toulouse, with streets named for Catholic saints, like Saint Peter and Saint Ann.

Bourbon Street, which was given its name in 1721, was named for the House of Bourbon, France's ruling family at the time. It's likely that bourbon, the spirit, was named after Bourbon Street, rather than the other way around, as it housed a bustling port where the drink sold well.

As historians Michael Veach and Chuck Cowdery have pointed out, that port only solidified the connection between Kentucky and New Orleans. By 1820, steamboat travel up and down the Mississippi River had become well established. These boats carried supplies, including lumber, construction materials, and, of course, Kentucky whiskey. The whiskey aged in barrels on the trip down, which, depending on the speed of the ship and its crew, could take between six and twenty-five days.

Once docked, the whiskey was sold as a kind of inexpensive stand-in for French brandy, which makes sense: Whiskey and brandy have similar notes of caramelized sugar, vanilla, and oak. Folks soon began to request "that Bourbon whiskey," referring to the street on which it was sold.

Modern-day distilleries still pay homage to the "spiritual" exchange between Kentucky and New Orleans. In 2017, Baton Rouge's Cane Land Distilling Company partnered with Kentucky's O. Z. Tyler Distillery (now Green River Distilling Company) to create their OMFW—Original Mississippi Floated Whiskey. The whiskey, which was described in a press release at the time as having a "bourbon mash bill," was shipped down the river. Once it finished its fourteen-day journey, it was stored in French cognac barrels until it was ready for distribution. A fitting tribute to the Kentucky–New Orleans connection.

Bourbon Street in New Orleans was named for the House of Bourbon, not after the spirit, which came later.

# BOURBON AND THE MISSISSIPPI RIVER

"Love makes the world go round? Not at all. Whisky makes it go round twice as fast."

—COMPTON MACKENZIE

There's a strong correlative relationship between the bourbon and steamboat trade industries. Geographically, Kentucky was perfectly positioned to both produce and distribute bourbon, thanks to the flowing limestone water that was incorporated in the mash, as well as the maze of tributaries and waterways connecting to the Mississippi River for trade. Kentuckian farmer-distillers would send barrels of bourbon by barge or steamboat down the Mississippi to New Orleans, where it would be greeted with open arms by the city's drinkers.

By the mid- to late-nineteenth century, demand for Kentucky whiskey had grown to such a degree that spirits merchants and distillers began to open shops in Louisville, a burgeoning port town. These shops tended to be on Main Street between about Oak and Tenth Streets, but also on Water Street to the north and Market Street to the south and on the connecting roads in between. This area quickly became known as Whiskey Row.

Whiskey Row was positioned close to the Ohio River because that was where the whiskey merchants did business with steamboats. Many distilleries were located nowhere close to Louisville but would keep an office near the port for meeting with potential customers. By the 1850s, there were more than thirty such businesses on Whiskey Row. Barrels were loaded onto steamboats that carried the valuable whiskey down the Ohio and often farther down the Mississippi River to their assigned destinations.

Some have posited that the gentle motion and sunlight the barrels were exposed to as they floated down the river positively impacted the flavor of the spirit within. One popular bourbon origin story is that a clear corn liquor was dumped into an oak barrel that lazily traveled down the Mississippi River to its final destination in New Orleans (presumably to be sold on Bourbon Street); when it was opened, much to everyone's pleasant surprise, it was not the clear distillate it had been at the start of its journey but a well-aged brown spirit that resembled today's bourbon.

Most bourbon historians agree that this probably isn't how it all went down, but the story of bourbon is undeniably connected to the Mississippi and those long-ago barrels, resting under the hot sun on a steamboat headed for New Orleans.

# BEAM
## The World's Finest Bourbon since 1795

# There are 167 years of Beam family history
## behind the good taste of Beam

In 1795 Jacob Beam settled in Kentucky and created the now famous Beam Bourbon formula. Today, Beam Bourbon is still being carefully distilled and aged according to the original formula by the 5th and 6th generations of the Beam family. That is why only Beam tastes like Beam . . . only Beam tastes so good.

# WORTHY OF YOUR TRUST

JIM BEAM 86 PROOF. ALL KENTUCKY STRAIGHT BOURBON WHISKIES DISTILLED AND BOTTLED BY THE JAMES B. BEAM DISTILLING CO., CLERMONT, BEAM, KENTUCKY.

BEAM'S CHOICE (Green label) Charcoal filtered, 6 years old (90 proof), sour mash bourbon with an unique good taste.

BEAM'S PIN BOTTLE Rare bottling of Kentucky Straight Bourbon, 8 and 10 years old (86.8 proof), with built-in pourer.

# TRUTH IN
# ADVERTISING

Soon after the repeal of Prohibition, bourbon brands began courting celebrity endorsements. In 1934, Schenley's Cream of Kentucky bourbon ran a series of *Life* magazine ads featuring a Norman Rockwell illustration of vaudeville star James Barton. The copy read: "As a great entertainer you, too, will score a real *hit*, if the next time you entertain, you serve your guests with the 'double-rich' Kentucky straight Bourbon!" The message was that bourbon enabled its purchaser to hold a great, sophisticated party, a promise that ads continued to make for the next several decades.

The 1960s saw a huge uptick in the number of big-name celebrities—Elliott Gould, Bette Davis, Sean Connery, and Henry Mancini among them—lending their faces to Jim Beam bourbon advertisements. Many of the distillery's ads appeared in *Playboy* magazine and presented the idea of "two one-of-a-kind originals"—the originals, of course, being the celebrity and the "world's finest bourbon."

During the 1970s, when bourbon's popularity plummeted, many distilleries began selling their product for cheaper and cheaper prices in order to compete with vodka's rising profile. By the 1980s, advertisers realized they needed to change tack. Bourbon's reputation needed a sophisticated makeover.

In an interview for Kentucky Bourbon Tales, a project conducted by the University of Kentucky's Louie B. Nunn Center for Oral History, Max Shapira, the president of Heaven Hill Distilleries, joked that "since the ending of Prohibition, as an industry, we've probably shot ourselves in the foot ten times. Then, finally, we started to do some things right. We introduced single barrels, small batches."

This advertisement for Jim Beam appeared in *Life* magazine in October 1961.

The advertising of this era made it explicit that bourbon was a luxury good. After Hiram Walker & Sons purchased Maker's Mark

**FOUR ROSES**

Old Fashioned Mellow Flavor

*Whiskey by Frankfort*

**FourRoses**
A BLEND OF STRAIGHT WHISKIES

QUALITY WHISKEY BY FRANKFORT

in 1981, the company quickly rolled out "upmarket advertising," with the tagline "It tastes expensive . . . and it is."

Today, the demographic of people drinking bourbon is expanding, and this is reflected in the advertising as well. While historic bourbon advertisements were incredibly white, male-oriented, and occasionally straight-up racist (as was the case with a pre-Prohibition advertisement for Paul Jones & Company that featured a "mammy" figure holding an absurdly large slice of watermelon and a Black man offering up a bottle of Paul Jones whiskey), that is changing. From Jack Daniel's establishing a partnership with the BET network to Jim Beam hiring Mila Kunis as a celebrity spokesperson to Samara Davis founding the Black Bourbon Society, advertisers, corporations, and consumers are responding to a world where bourbon has become more inclusive and diverse.

# What Lobster did for Maine, Old Crow did for Bourbon.

The good taste of Lobster put Maine on the map. The good taste of Old Crow made Bourbon famous.

Before 1835, Bourbon was made every which way. That year, Dr. James Crow took it out of the hit-or-miss league and invented the process that gave Bourbon its mellow taste—and good name: Old Crow.

OLD CROW

86 PROOF
4/5 QUART

OLD CROW

*Kentucky*
STRAIGHT BOURBON
WHISKEY

DISTILLED AND BOTTLED
UNDER UNITED STATES GOVERNMENT SUPERVISION BY

*W. A. Gaines*
DIVISION OF
THE OLD CROW DISTILLERY COMPANY
FRANKFORT. KY. · LOUISVILLE. KY.

# LEXINGTON AND ENVIRONS

If Louisville is the industrial center of Kentucky, Lexington is the picturesque city of history and tradition. A proper bourbon tour is not complete without a visit to this beautiful city, home of the pristine Keeneland Racetrack, where you can watch Thoroughbreds race on an oval track all day long in hopes of betting on the winning horse. Or you can spend the day tasting through the city's lively distilleries. (I think you know which one I would choose.)

Lexington is the hub of the craft bourbon industry, and in many ways, it's where bourbon is heading. Start at **BARREL HOUSE DISTILLING CO.** in the city's historic distillery district, where you can sample some honest bourbons that you won't find in your home state. At **BLUEGRASS DISTILLERS**, pretty much the entire team was homegrown in Lexington. This is becoming rare in an industry that is exploding, as more and more people flock to Kentucky to reap the profits bourbon promises. While there's nothing wrong with outside influences per se, at the end of the day, hometown people are motivated by something more than just dollars. You can feel this sentiment all over Lexington.

Before Prohibition, there were hundreds of bourbon distilleries in Kentucky. During

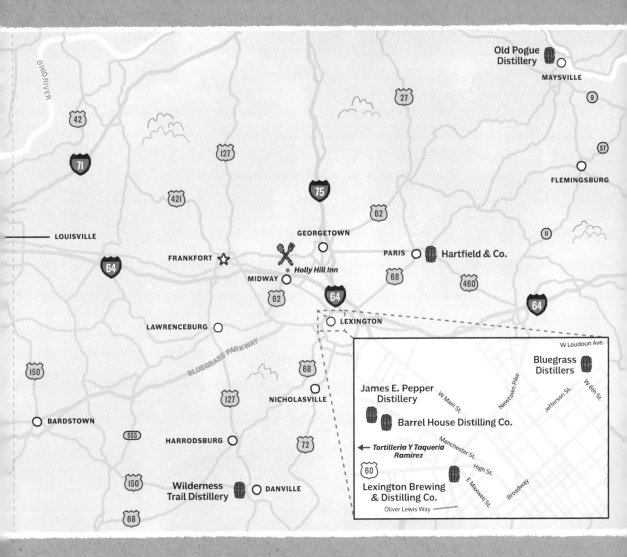

the dark ages of bourbon after Prohibition, World War II, and the vodka craze of the 1980s, many great distilleries and labels went out of business. An effort is underway to revive some of these whiskeys, and a prime example of this is **JAMES E. PEPPER DISTILLERY**. Colonel James E. Pepper was a bourbon industrialist of the late 1800s, and his family's history is on full display at the distillery. Sip on some of the best rye whiskey around and take a history lesson on bourbon at the same time. **LEXINGTON BREWING & DISTILLING CO.** is a bit of a misnomer for a bourbon company. They do make beer, aging some in bourbon barrels, but they also make Town Branch—one of my favorite bourbons— and if they have the single-barrel available, stock up.

Now, lest I paint a picture of Lexington that's all white picket fences and corn dogs, I will let you in on a secret about this city—it has some of the best Mexican restaurants I have been to anywhere in the United States, and the best of them is Tortilleria Y Taqueria Ramirez, where you can watch them make their homemade tortillas. I am partial to a lengua taco (that's beef tongue) and a comforting bowl of pozole, a pork and hominy soup.

It's a short drive on US 68 East from Lexington to Paris, Kentucky, at the heart of Bourbon County, one of Kentucky's original nine counties. Obviously, this county gets its name from its historic ties to bourbon, but after Prohibition, none of its distilleries reopened. Until recently, there was no distillery tour stop in Bourbon County, a glaring irony that has always struck me as both comedic and tragic. In 2014, **HARTFIELD & CO.** opened a distillery in the heart of Bourbon County and has dedicated itself to making pre-Prohibition-style bourbons. I leave it up to the pundits to argue what "pre-Prohibition-style bourbon" means, but I can attest that it's wonderful bourbon and worth a visit.

One of the first bourbons I fell in love with when I arrived in Kentucky over twenty years ago was Old Pogue from the **OLD POGUE DISTILLERY** in Maysville. It was so different from the large-production bourbons I was accustomed to, and it had a long and legendary history. This distillery is a bit out of the way, but if you truly want to understand the birthplace of bourbon and a legacy that started before the Civil War, take a trip to Maysville (which, at one point, was part of Virginia). Nowadays, it's difficult for me to get my hands on a bottle, but that's okay. I'm happy for the people at Old Pogue and all the other small producers who have found success in this bourbon renaissance.

On your way back to Lexington, you'll hear your stomach grumbling for some evening victuals. Chef Ouita Michel is the unofficial mayor of the city, and a visit to any of her numerous restaurants will guarantee you a fine supper. But if you want to experience the one that started it all, make a reservation at Holly Hill Inn in Midway, Kentucky. I've eaten there more than I've eaten at any other restaurant in my life, and it amazingly just keeps getting better.

The last stop is a bit south of Lexington, sitting alone in the pristine town of Danville. **WILDERNESS TRAIL DISTILLERY** makes a critically acclaimed bourbon that is surprisingly well crafted for such a young operation. But it comes as no surprise when you learn that this place is also the home of Ferm Solutions and its co-owner Pat Heist, who have been cultivating yeast strains for bourbon distilleries for years. It's no wonder, then, that Wilderness Trail is making some of the most accomplished bourbons in the state.

# BOURBON-GLAZED CHICKEN WINGS

Chicken wings are one of the most iconic dishes in American cuisine. (I read somewhere that the average American will consume about 18,000 chicken wings in a lifetime.) So I wanted to create a recipe for chicken wings that uses the one truly American spirit: bourbon. They're a classic combination. This recipe is a golden egg of a recipe—a sticky bourbon-soy-glazed delight of a wing. Make sure to use whole chicken wings because they have more surface area for the sauce to cling to.

**Serves 6 as an appetizer**

**FOR THE WINGS**

4 pounds whole chicken wings

2 tablespoons canola oil

1 tablespoon smoked paprika

1 tablespoon kosher salt

1½ teaspoons granulated sugar

**FOR THE GLAZE**

2 cups bourbon

½ cup sorghum syrup

½ cup brown sugar

¼ cup apple cider vinegar

¼ cup Tabasco

2 tablespoons soy sauce

¼ cup crushed toasted peanuts, for garnish

½ bunch scallions, thinly sliced, for garnish

Position a rack in the upper third of the oven. Preheat the oven to 400°F.

To make the wings, in a large bowl, toss the wings with the canola oil, paprika, salt, and granulated sugar until evenly coated. Let the wings sit at room temperature while you prepare the glaze.

To make the glaze, in a medium saucepan, whisk together the bourbon, sorghum, brown sugar, vinegar, Tabasco, and soy sauce. Bring the mixture to a boil over medium-high heat and cook for about 15 minutes, until the liquid has reduced to a thin syrup. Remove from the heat and let cool.

« CONTINUED »

Meanwhile, arrange the wings on a sheet pan in an even layer. Bake for 20 minutes, then increase the oven temperature to 450°F. Flip the wings and bake for 10 minutes more; they should be cooked through at this point. The wing bone should easily pull out of the meat and the skin should be golden brown.

Transfer the wings to a large bowl (reserve the sheet pan; you're going to use it again). Pour the glaze over the wings and toss to evenly coat, then return them to the sheet pan. Pour any remaining glaze over the wings and bake for 10 minutes more, until sticky and lightly charred.

Return the wings and any liquid on the sheet pan to the bowl with the glaze. Toss again to evenly coat the wings with the glaze. Arrange the wings on a platter and sprinkle with the toasted peanuts and sliced scallions before serving.

# BOURBON AND GOCHUJANG BBQ SHRIMP

When I think about who I am and what I love, I don't know if there's a better representation of my culinary identity than the marriage of Korean gochujang and Kentucky bourbon in a barbecue sauce that's full of punch. Bourbon is such a great pairing with chile because it can hold up to spiciness without getting overpowered.

**Serves 4**

1 cup apple cider vinegar

1 cup bourbon

1 cup ketchup

½ cup brown sugar

¼ cup brewed coffee

1 tablespoon gochujang

1 tablespoon Worcestershire sauce

1 tablespoon onion powder

2 teaspoons garlic powder

Kosher salt and freshly ground black pepper

24 shrimp (preferably jumbo), peeled and deveined

1 (12-ounce) bag tortilla chips

1 jalapeño, thinly sliced, for garnish

In a medium pot, combine the vinegar, bourbon, ketchup, brown sugar, coffee, gochujang, Worcestershire, onion powder, garlic powder, and salt and pepper to taste. Bring to a simmer over medium-low heat, then cook for 45 minutes, until the sauce thickens. Let cool to room temperature.

Place the shrimp in a large bowl and add 1 cup of the barbecue sauce. Let marinate in the fridge for 30 minutes.

Heat a grill to high or warm a cast-iron skillet over high heat.

Drain the shrimp from the marinade and grill until fully cooked and pink, about 3 minutes.

Place some tortilla chips in a bowl, top with the grilled shrimp, and drizzle more barbecue sauce over the shrimp. Garnish with a few slices of fresh jalapeño and serve.

# QUAIL WITH ROASTED BANANA BBQ SAUCE

Who says barbecue has to always involve Neanderthal slabs of fatty meat? Don't sleep on barbecued quail. The rich, gamy, and fragrant quail flesh can more than handle a vinegar- and spice-forward barbecue sauce. Try to find semi-boneless quail, which means that the bones have been removed from the breasts but the legs still have their bones.

### Serves 2 as an appetizer

2 whole quail (see headnote)

2 teaspoons unsalted butter, melted

½ teaspoon sea salt

Pinch of freshly ground black pepper

½ cup Roasted Banana BBQ Sauce
(recipe follows)

**SPECIAL EQUIPMENT**

Twine

Preheat the oven to 425°F.

Crisscross the ends of the quail legs and tie them together with a little kitchen twine. Brush the entire quail with the melted butter and sprinkle with the salt and pepper.

Place the quail in a roasting pan and roast for about 12 minutes. Remove the quail from the oven and brush with the BBQ sauce, then return them to the oven and roast for 4 minutes more, until the skin is browned and the meat is cooked through and reaches an internal temperature of 155°F. Let the quail rest for 3 minutes before serving. Cut off and discard the twine from the legs.

Serve the quail on a plate with additional BBQ sauce on the side.

« CONTINUED »

# ROASTED BANANA BBQ SAUCE

Not sure what to do with overripe bananas? Try this barbecue sauce. Once banana is roasted and pureed with an assortment of spices, its tropical flavor gives way to an earthy creaminess that makes a wonderful base for a complex barbecue sauce. Try it on lamb, pheasant, rabbit, or any other gamy meat.

**Makes 2 cups**

4 ripe large bananas (in their skins)

2 tablespoons vegetable oil

½ cup finely chopped onion

2 garlic cloves, minced

2 teaspoons grated fresh ginger

1 teaspoon mustard powder

½ teaspoon cayenne pepper

½ teaspoon smoked paprika

½ teaspoon ground turmeric

¼ teaspoon ground allspice

1 cup bourbon

¾ cup apple cider vinegar

3 tablespoons soy sauce

2½ tablespoons dark brown sugar

2 tablespoons tamarind paste

1½ tablespoons tomato paste

1 tablespoon spicy mustard

1 teaspoon kosher salt, plus more
  if needed

Preheat the oven to 400°F.

Arrange the whole bananas, still in their skins, in a single layer on a sheet pan. Roast for 20 to 25 minutes, until blackened and very soft. Set aside to cool.

In a medium pot, heat the oil over medium heat. Add the onion and cook, stirring occasionally, until softened, about 5 minutes. Add the garlic, ginger, mustard powder, cayenne, paprika, turmeric, and allspice. Cook for 1 minute, stirring continuously. Add the bourbon and bring to a boil, then simmer vigorously for 3 minutes, or until the bourbon has reduced by half.

Peel the bananas and add them to the pot, along with any juices from the sheet pan. Coarsely mash the bananas with a wooden spoon. Stir in the vinegar, soy sauce, brown sugar, tamarind paste, tomato paste, spicy mustard, and salt. Bring to a simmer. Reduce the heat to low, cover the pan, and cook, stirring often, for 15 minutes. Remove from the heat and let cool for 5 minutes.

Transfer the cooled mixture to a blender and blend until smooth, about 1 minute.

Taste and season with salt, if needed. Return the sauce to the pot and simmer for 3 minutes. Transfer the sauce to a jar and let cool to room temperature. Store in the fridge for up to 3 weeks.

# BLACKENED SALMON WITH BOURBON-SOY MARINADE, BOK CHOY, AND GREEN APPLE

I want people to think of bourbon as more than just a sidekick to beef and pork. Bourbon has a softer side; it's spice-forward, with notes of leather and hay that accentuate the flavors in fatty fish like salmon, trout, cod, and halibut. Blackening is a great way to add charred notes to fish, and bourbon will always be a friend to round out those flavors.

**Serves 2 as a main**

### FOR THE BOURBON-SOY MARINADE

I cup bourbon, reduced to ½ cup (see page 75)

½ cup honey

¼ cup soy sauce

I teaspoon fish sauce

I teaspoon fresh lemon juice

½ teaspoon freshly ground black pepper

### FOR THE SALMON

2 (6-ounce) boneless, skinless salmon fillets

I tablespoon olive oil

4 tablespoons (½ stick) unsalted butter

¼ cup bourbon

2 teaspoons soy sauce

4 heads baby bok choy

½ green apple, cored and sliced into matchsticks

I red Thai chile, thinly sliced

To make the bourbon-soy marinade, in a medium bowl, mix together the reduced bourbon, honey, soy sauce, fish sauce, lemon juice, and pepper.

To prepare the salmon, place it in a zip-top plastic bag and add the marinade. Close the bag, removing as much air as possible. Marinate in the fridge for 1 hour.

In a cast-iron skillet, heat the olive oil over medium heat. Remove the salmon from the bag and discard the marinade. Pat the salmon dry with a paper towel. Add the salmon to the skillet and sear until blackened on the bottom, about 3 minutes.

**« CONTINUED »**

Flip the salmon, reduce the heat to medium-low, and cook for 5 minutes more, until it reaches medium-rare (120°F on an instant-read thermometer). Turn off the heat and let the salmon rest in the pan for 3 minutes.

In a separate sauté pan, melt the butter over medium heat. Let the butter bubble and brown slightly, about 2 minutes. Add the bourbon and soy sauce and simmer for 1 minute.

Meanwhile, cut off the stem ends of the bok choy and separate the leaves. Add the bok choy leaves to the pan and sauté for 1 minute, until the bok choy is just cooked and the sauce has reduced.

Place the salmon on a plate. Top with the bok choy and garnish with the apple matchsticks. Add a few thin slices of the Thai chile. Pour the bourbon sauce over the salmon and serve right away.

# PORK MEATBALLS
# IN BOURBON-GOCHUJANG COCONUT BROTH

I would never, ever admit to having a favorite recipe, but, well, having said that, this recipe is pretty damn near the top of my list. Pork, bourbon, and gochujang all play important roles in this rollicking dish of layered tastes. The coconut milk is the secret star, though, bridging all the disparate ingredients.

**Serves 4 as a main**

### FOR THE MEATBALLS

I pound ground pork

I (2-inch) piece fresh ginger, peeled and minced

3 garlic cloves, minced

I large egg

1/3 cup panko bread crumbs

2 tablespoons bourbon

2 tablespoons chopped fresh cilantro stems, leaves reserved for garnish

1 1/2 teaspoons soy sauce

1 1/2 teaspoons fish sauce

1/2 teaspoon kosher salt

1/4 teaspoon freshly ground black pepper

Canola oil

### FOR THE BROTH

2 cups chicken stock

7 ounces unsweetened coconut milk

1/2 cup bourbon

2 tablespoons gochujang

I tablespoon soy sauce

I teaspoon sugar

2 garlic cloves, lightly smashed

I (1/2-inch) piece fresh ginger, peeled and lightly smashed

### FOR THE CUCUMBER AND RADISH SALAD

I English cucumber, thinly sliced

3 red radishes, thinly sliced

3/4 teaspoon kosher salt

1 1/2 tablespoons rice vinegar

1 1/2 teaspoons toasted sesame seeds

1/2 teaspoon sugar

### TO SERVE

4 cups cooked rice

I lime, cut into wedges

To make the meatballs, in a large bowl, combine the pork, ginger, garlic, egg, panko, bourbon, cilantro stems, soy sauce, fish sauce, salt, and pepper. Using your hands, mix gently until all the ingredients are evenly distributed. Roll the meat mixture into balls, using about 1 1/2 tablespoons for each.

**« CONTINUED »**

Heat a cast-iron pan over medium heat. Add a little canola oil and sear the meatballs until brown on all sides, about 2 minutes per side. Transfer the browned meatballs to a plate and set aside until the broth is ready.

To make the broth, in a small pot, whisk together the stock, coconut milk, bourbon, gochujang, soy sauce, sugar, garlic, and ginger. Bring to a boil, then reduce the heat to maintain a simmer and cook for 15 minutes, until the liquid has reduced by half. Add the meatballs to the broth and simmer over medium heat for 6 minutes.

Meanwhile, to make the cucumber and radish salad, in a small bowl, combine the cucumber and radishes. Sprinkle the salt over the top and let stand at room temperature for 5 minutes to draw out the moisture. Squeeze and drain the liquid from the vegetables, discarding any excess liquid in the bowl, too. Add the vinegar, sesame seeds, and sugar to the bowl and toss everything together.

Divide the rice among four bowls. Add the meatballs and a good bit of the broth. Garnish each bowl with the cucumber and radish salad, cilantro leaves, and a wedge of lime. Serve immediately.

# GRILLED CHICKEN THIGHS
# IN A HONEY, MISO, AND MUSTARD MARINADE

Bourbon and grilling are a match whose foundation is rooted in the charred flavor essential to both. High heat and smoke seem to intensify the bourbon flavor in the marinade, and chicken is the perfect base for this dish. Serve the chicken simply on a bed of broccoli rabe that soaks up the sauce. Try this with a well-aged bourbon on ice with a splash of water, and see for yourself how the pairing brings out the flavors in the browned chicken.

**Serves 2 as a main**

FOR THE MARINADE

¼ cup dark miso paste

¼ cup bourbon

2 tablespoons brown mustard

2 tablespoons honey

I tablespoon rice vinegar

I teaspoon soy sauce

FOR THE CHICKEN

2 boneless chicken thighs

I pound broccoli rabe

2 garlic cloves, minced

2 tablespoons olive oil

Kosher salt and freshly ground
   black pepper

To make the marinade, in a large bowl, combine the miso, bourbon, mustard, honey, vinegar, and soy sauce. Save a little marinade in a separate small bowl to use as a finishing sauce later.

To prepare the chicken, place it in the bowl with the marinade and cover with plastic wrap. Marinate the chicken in the fridge for 1 hour.

Heat a grill to high or heat a cast-iron skillet over medium-high heat.

In a medium bowl, combine the broccoli rabe, garlic, and olive oil. Season with salt and pepper and set aside.

« CONTINUED »

Remove the chicken from the marinade and pat dry (you can discard the chicken marinade). Grill the chicken skin-side down for about 3 minutes, until the skin is caramelized and browned, then flip the chicken and grill until the flesh is cooked through, about 8 minutes, then remove from the grill.

Place the broccoli rabe on the grill and cook for 4 minutes, until charred and cooked through. Remove from the grill.

Arrange the broccoli rabe on a platter and top with the chicken thighs. Drizzle a little of the reserved marinade over the chicken and broccoli rabe. Serve right away.

# YEAST AND UMAMI

Somewhere in the flavor wheel of bourbon (see page 196), past the caramel and tobacco, the dried figs and hay, somewhere in the corners of your mouth, in the hidden places in between, there are the minor notes, quietly prominent beneath the surface. It could be a faint whiff of river moss or a macerated rose petal or a bruised strawberry with a hint of gravel. It could just be your mind playing tricks on you, or it could be something happening on a molecular level, impossible for you to comprehend in the same way that you can touch and feel a stave of oak, an ear of corn, or a handful of barley.

Pat Heist's office at Ferm Solutions in Danville, Kentucky, is filled with hundreds of sample bourbon recipes and barrel picks in pint-size glass bottles marked with handwritten notes. I talk to Pat about the part of bourbon that's invisible to the naked eye. We discuss yeast and bacteria and how they affect taste in bourbon on a cellular level. This is different from touring a cooperage or watching a field of corn grow. With Pat, it's just the two of us on leather couches, surrounded by seemingly endless variations on the flavor of bourbon.

Ferm Solutions is a company that creates yeast strains for the beverage world, everything from bourbon to beer to kombucha. If there's fermentation involved, Pat can help you make your beverage better. His company is essentially one of the world's only spirit and beer yeast repositories, cataloging, creating, modifying, and fixing yeast strains for thousands of beverage companies globally. There are several chest freezers filled with boxes that each hold hundreds of small vials, within which are the secret yeast strains for all your favorite bourbons, held in stasis at −80°C.

Yeast isn't talked about much in the world of bourbon. It doesn't have the visuals of fire or the romance of ancient rivers or the tactile resonance of oak trees, but without yeast, you can't have fermentation, and without fermentation, there's no whiskey. Some would argue that yeast is just the agent that kicks off the necessary chemical reaction to convert sugar into alcohol. But a

statement like that gets Pat furrowing his eyebrows and going red in the face. He's a fount of scientific knowledge, delivered in a rapid Kentucky drawl. He's got a long white beard reminiscent of Scott Ian's. (There's a reason for the rock star beard: He's also the lead singer in a heavy metal band.)

Pat tells me everything I need to know about yeast: "It is a living organism. The one we use for bourbon is *Saccharomyces cerevisiae*, the same yeast you would use in baking. But the similarities to baking end there, because your understanding of yeast as a chef is different from a distiller's." That's because in distillation, the purpose of yeast is to convert sugar into alcohol, not act as a leavening agent. Distillers use yeast that is highly attenuated, meaning it will use up more of the sugar and yield more alcohol.

So how does yeast influence the final flavor of a bourbon? "Yeast makes alcohol," says Pat. "Not just ethyl alcohol—there are traces of other alcohols like propanol, methanol, and butanol in much smaller quantities, but these alcohols all have flavors. Another important thing that yeast provides is organic acids, which, later on, become esters. Once the alcohol is in the barrel, there is an extraction of chemicals from the barrel; some are water-soluble, and some are alcohol-soluble. With each cycle of expansion and contraction, there are chemical reactions that happen over time. Depending on the length of carbon on the esters, you'll get different flavors, anything from nutmeg to rose petal. Now, the yeast isn't creating those flavors because the yeast is long gone at this point, but the chemicals that the yeast produced are present and creating chemical reactions in the barrel."

In every conversation I have with Pat, I find myself begging him to slow down and start at the beginning. As a chef, when I think about yeast, the image of warm toasty sourdoughs and nutty brioches come to mind. To me, yeast is something you buy in small square envelopes and mix with tepid water to create rise in doughs. In bourbon, this would be the equivalent to the corn mash reacting with the just-added yeast bubbling in an open-air tank. Pat reminds me that the corn mash at this stage tastes and smells like farina or cornbread. But distillers don't stop here—they keep going until the yeast has consumed all the sugar and converted it into alcohol. How much yeast and what strain and what rate of consumption are what Pat figures out for each distillery.

Pat shows me how he can capture yeast strains on petri dishes in his backyard or culture them on pieces of fruit. He shows me what they look like under a microscope. He traces their origins back hundreds of millions of years to the beginning of life on earth. All this is informative, but it's still hard to comprehend something you cannot see.

"We've only known about yeast from a microscopic level for the last few hundred years," says Pat. "But humans have been making alcohol and wine and soured foods for thousands of years. We have always had this relationship with yeast and bacteria. We just didn't know what it was. Now I can cultivate and catalog and accurately tell you what yeasts you need for certain kinds of bourbon. You can figure it out on your own, but I got all the strains right here, and I already know which ones you want."

There are so many variables in making bourbon that it's impossible to isolate what yeast contributes to in terms of flavor in a bottle of bourbon, but there's no denying that it's there. Like so many other aspects of bourbon, there's a science and an art to it. For all the laboratory work at the core of Ferm Solutions, to hear Pat talk for hours about yeast and bacteria is to listen to a poetic dissertation on the origins of life on earth.

"We have over ten thousand strains of yeasts and over one hundred thousand strains of bacteria. People think they know everything about making bourbon, but a lot of it is still a mystery," says Pat. "Yeast is the key to unlocking a lot of flavors that we can't control or even identify. So much happens in the grain fermentation that will affect flavor: your grain-to-water ratio, how fast you ferment, how coarse your grain is, even the bacteria floating around in your distillery." Pat and I taste through bottle after bottle of different bourbons, and I can smell and taste different floral notes, from wildflowers to sandalwood to something akin to a sweaty (albeit slightly pleasant) armpit. He tells me that the only difference in these various bourbons is the yeast strain. It is an eye-opening experience.

At Pat's lab, I am struck by a magnified image of a round mother yeast cell forming a bud cell on its side. Pat explains that yeast can multiply at astounding rates, which makes it so ideal for alcohol production. He tells me that scientists are researching aging in humans by comparing our cells to yeast cells because they're so similar. A mother yeast cell will bud a daughter cell that will grow and

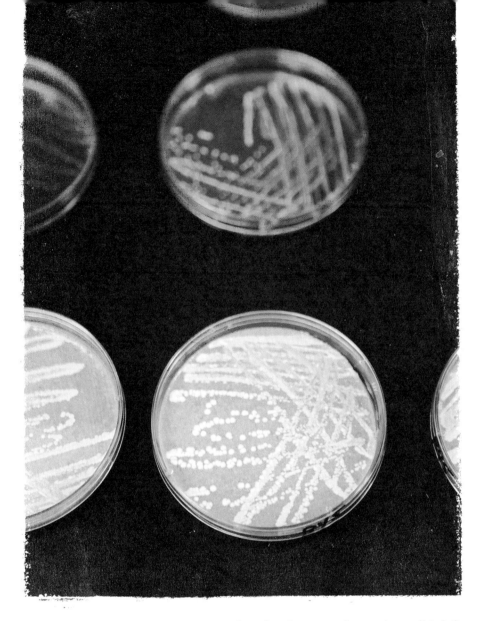

eventually detach from its mother. When that happens, the mother cell is left with a bud scar where the daughter detached. You can tell the age of a mother cell by how many scars she has on her surface. She will reproduce as much as she can, relentlessly multiplying and forming new scars, until she has too many scars to bud, signifying the end of her life cycle.

Learning this hits me with a wave of sadness for this single-celled microorganism; without a brain or a heart or consciousness, it still accomplishes everything we ask of it, only to sacrifice its life for the sake of our golden bourbon.

# GOLD RUSH

The Gold Rush is a simple and beloved drink, but in the hands of a technical and creative wizard like Eron Plevan, one of Louisville's most skilled cocktail makers, it becomes elevated to a signature cocktail that has won him loyal fans all over Louisville.

**Makes 1**

1½ ounces bourbon

¾ ounce fresh lemon juice

¾ ounce Salted Orange Blossom
  Honey Syrup (recipe follows)

½ ounce Golden Raisin Lemonade
  (recipe follows)

Pour the bourbon, lemon juice, honey syrup, and lemonade into a cocktail shaker with ice. Shake for 10 to 15 seconds. Strain over a large ice cube into a cocktail glass or coupe.

> "My favorite thing is the ability to use the bar as a platform to give back. Whether that means curating a cocktail menu that raises proceeds for a worthy cause or training new bartenders to set them up for long-term success, there are so many opportunities for a bar to be bigger than drinks."
>
> **—ERON PLEVAN**

« CONTINUED »

# SALTED ORANGE BLOSSOM HONEY SYRUP

**Makes 2 cups**

1½ cups honey

½ cup hot water

¾ teaspoon kosher salt

½ teaspoon orange blossom water

In a small pot, combine the honey, hot water, and salt. Cook over low heat, stirring, for 5 minutes, until combined. Let cool to room temperature, then mix in the orange blossom water. Store in a covered jar in the fridge for up to 2 weeks.

# GOLDEN RAISIN LEMONADE

**Makes 2 cups**

2 lemons, washed and sliced into thin wheels

1 cup dark brown sugar

1 cup granulated sugar

½ cup golden raisins

6½ cups hot (not boiling) water

In a sanitized container, combine the lemons, both sugars, and the raisins and shake to generously coat the lemons and raisins with the sugar. Let sit for 40 minutes to allow the sugars to extract the essential oils and juice from the lemon slices. Add the hot water to the container and stir until all the sugar has dissolved, about 2 minutes. Let cool to room temperature, about 30 minutes, then strain into a bottle. Store in the fridge for up to 2 weeks.

# BOURBON AND UMAMI

"The light music of whisky falling into glasses made an agreeable interlude."
—JAMES JOYCE

"Umami" is a word we use to describe the funky, earthy flavors in foods like soy sauce, mushrooms, and chocolate. A lot of umami flavors, like those in fish sauce and miso, are developed through fermentation. It wouldn't be accurate to describe the fermentation that happens in bourbon as resulting in an umami flavor, since most culinary fermentation is bacterial and, as we already know, the function of yeast in distilling is different from its function in baking (see page 181). But there are some things at work here that make me think about the umami qualities of bourbon. When I think about fermented products like soy sauce or country ham, there seems to be a connection to bourbon in that all of them grow more complex as they age. Though the yeast is no longer there inside the barrels, the acids that are present as a result of the yeast are reacting with the oak and the char and the passage of time. When someone presses me for a definition of umami, I always say it's like tasting the passage of time. And so it is with bourbon: With each passing year, the depth and layers grow, the esters lengthen, the aroma fills a room longer, the color turns amber, then gold.

This also means that bourbon is great for pairing with foods that have strong fermented flavors, especially the ones that are aggressive and salty. Foods like miso, fermented black beans, stinky washed-rind cheeses, and chocolate are all umami-rich. Traditionally, pairing beverages with these assertive flavors has been challenging, but bourbon offers a versatile solution. It's strong enough to stand its ground against even the most pungent flavors while still preserving its own sweet and savory notes.

# THE CRITIC

# FRED MINNICK

Fred Minnick published his first story in the *Oklahoma County News* at age fifteen. He has written about a variety of subjects over his career and eventually found his passion as a bourbon writer. He has written three books and countless articles on bourbon, hosts a bourbon podcast, serves as a judge for bourbon competitions, emcees various bourbon tastings around the country, and generally lives and breathes all things bourbon. When I'm stuck on a piece of bourbon history or a tasting note, Fred is the first person I contact. Every art form needs a champion, and for bourbon, that champion is Fred. He has amplified the gospel of bourbon with educated analysis, tasting acumen, sound criticism, and unrivaled dedication.

**Q:** *How do you like your bourbon?*

**A:** Usually neat. But if I am at a concert or a ball game, I will throw a cube in there, so it's both refreshing and delicious but not forcing me to go into critic mode.

**Q:** *How did you get into bourbon writing and ranking bourbons?*

**A:** When I returned home from serving in Iraq in 2005, I entered the freelance writing business, moved to Kentucky, and jumped into therapy to help cope with my war trauma. I had always been a bourbon fan, but I didn't realize I had a skill for both smelling and tasting. It was when my therapist introduced me to taste mindfulness that I discovered I could taste things others did not. That focus on my tongue really changed my life. Around 2008, I started writing my tasting notes. Over the years, I added scores, but I never really liked scoring bourbon, because people would skip right over the tasting notes. So I dropped scores in 2018 and started ranking bourbon or naming "best of" categories. To me, pitting one bourbon against another is a more accurate way of picking your favorite. I am just one taster and you should taste for yourself.

**Q:** *Is bourbon better now than it was twenty years ago? Where will it be twenty years from now?*

**A:** Bourbon's dropped the old-school mantra that nothing can be done to it. So today, we have people thinking a port-finished bourbon is a "bourbon," which it's not. And you have people thinking a blend of straight bourbon is bourbon, which it's not. They are a distilled spirit specialty and blend of straights, respectively, and that never would have happened when old-timers were running the show. New blood has brought in so many techniques from Scotch and wine that it's opened up the flavor profiles. But it's also a dangerous situation in that products considered bourbon are not exactly living up to the standards. I am a curmudgeon on this, and I genuinely like the new flavors, but I wish they would label them as "whiskey" and not "bourbon." On the positive side, the plethora of small distillers dropping well-aged bourbon will bring bourbon to another level of flavors over the next twenty years. Today, we are seeing distillers not shy away from grain flavors or low-proof entries, which can give a more buttery mouthfeel. I can't wait for the next two decades.

**Q:** *What is vintage bourbon, and do you have a favorite one?*

**A:** A bourbon made before 1994 is the optimal time to start considering it a vintage whiskey. GMO grains were introduced in 1994. And while not all distillers switched to GMOs, enough did over time to make a substantial difference in the corn being used. My favorite vintage pour of all time is a 1960s-era Old Crow chess piece. I had a taste that I can close my eyes and still feel it dropping down my jawline. It was heavenly.

# HOW TO TASTE
# BOURBON LIKE A PRO

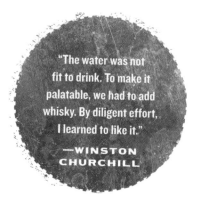

"The water was not fit to drink. To make it palatable, we had to add whisky. By diligent effort, I learned to like it."

**—WINSTON CHURCHILL**

Fred Minnick has the job you wish you could have: He tastes and rates bourbon for a living. His books are essential reading for any bourbon aficionado, and his mission to popularize bourbon through his podcast, his writings, and his reviews has been instrumental in creating the professional yet relaxed culture of bourbon that is so unique in the beverage world. His answers to three simple questions will change the way you taste bourbon:

### I. What do you look for when tasting a bourbon?

When reviewing a whiskey, I'm first looking for flaws. Does it have any off notes? Notes like turpentine, rotten apples, sweaty gym socks, and nail polish come from bad distillation. Then I look for developmental notes. These are the

notes from the ingredients and how they've aged. For example, a young bourbon will have a great deal of corn and wood in it, but as it ages, these notes soften and are less pronounced. If a bourbon is eight years old and tastes like corn on the cob, that's often a sign of a slow-aging barrel. Then I focus on my tongue. How does it feel? How long is it on there? It's at this point that you're really paying attention to how the whiskey moves on the tongue. Does it come in like an ocean wave or a trickle from a faucet? I analyze what part of the tongue it's most prominent on and laser in on the flavors. And finally, how long does it finish? Meaning, after I've swallowed, what is the most prominent flavor left and how long is it there?

**2. How do you know one bourbon is better than another, especially since most bourbons are similar in flavor profile?**

I sort of have a mental checklist that downgrades with every flaw and developmental note that I find unappealing. But what really separates bourbons for me are what I call "points on the palate." This is how many parts of the tongue the bourbon lights up. The more, the better. And if two bourbons hit the same amount of points on the palate, I go with the one with the longer finish, meaning how long it's still on the tongue. If that's equal, well, I guess it's dependent upon my mood, and this is where personal preference makes its play. Some days I prefer a rich jalapeño pepper spice over a caramel chew. And sometimes I crave the corn-bread note. The craziest thing is that my personal preference and even the performance of my tongue will vary from day to day. Tasting is a lot like athletic endeavors. Some days you perform better than others.

**3. Where do the different flavors of bourbon come from?**

There are many sources of flavor. Materials: grain, yeast, water, and wood. Execution technique: fermentation, distillation, aging, and proofing water. All that being said, the two most dominant flavor creators are the yeast and the barrel, followed by grains and techniques. And if you had to pick just one flavor creator, it would be the barrel. Something magical happens in that new charred oak barrel sitting in a warehouse. And to be honest, science still cannot fully explain why two barrels filled on the exact same day sitting next to each other for ten years can taste so uniquely different. I think that's why I love tasting bourbon so much: The variables cannot be defined. I like the art more than the science.

# HOW TO PAIR BOURBON
# FOR A DINNER PARTY

If you want to be the life of your next dinner party, try doing a bourbon-themed meal. If you've been paying attention to the recipes in this book, it's safe to say you're learning a thing or two about how to cook with bourbon and how to pair an array of diverse foods with your favorite bourbons. But it gets trickier when you're throwing a dinner party with several courses paired with bourbon.

Because of bourbon's high proof, it would not be wise to serve a neat glass of bourbon with each course at dinner, unless your goal is to have a rowdy food fight by the dessert course. A better method is to ease your guests along a journey of bourbon as the dinner progresses. Here are some rules to guide you:

- Cocktails are an essential way to lower the proof of your libation while still serving bourbon. There are endless cocktails to choose from and a panorama of flavors that can pair with your dinner ingredients.

- Start with lighter-proof cocktails and progress toward heavier ones. If you start with a Manhattan, you have nowhere else to go, so start with something light, like a Gold Rush (page 187) or simply a bourbon with club soda, before getting into anything heavier.

- Your beverage should never be sweeter than your food. This applies to wine, whiskey, mocktails—any beverage pairing. Your mouth will adjust to the sweetest thing that hits your tongue, so if you pair a sweet cocktail with a savory course, your food will taste bland. Stay away from cocktails that are too fruity or sweet until the last course.

- Start the evening with your best bourbon, end with bottom-shelf swill. I've been to many bourbon dinners where they waited until the last course or, even worse, after dinner to break out the twenty-year bourbon. By then,

the nuances were lost on me. After multiple courses of food and countless drinks, you should be reaching for an antacid, not a fine spirit. If you want to impress your guests with a rare and nuanced bourbon, do it at the beginning of the meal, when their palates are fresh. Add an option of water or club soda to lighten the proof, and keep it simple. Saving the best for last doesn't always work when it comes to bourbon dinners.

- Lastly, keep it fun. Bourbon is a great conversation starter. I've never been to a quiet bourbon dinner. Let your guests have fun. No one loves a fifteen-minute lecture on how incredibly expensive your bourbon collection is. The bourbon will speak for itself. Nothing dampens a lively dinner more than a host who boasts about the rarity of a bourbon at the start of each course.

# THE BOURBON
# FLAVOR WHEEL

How do you describe the bourbon you're drinking? Is it smooth or harsh? Is it sweet or spicy? Does it taste of tobacco or orange peel? Is this all made up in your head, or is there a real science behind the flavors you taste when you sip bourbon? While many bars and distilleries have their own flavor wheels to which they refer when describing their bourbon, one of the easiest models to comprehend, especially for new drinkers, is the American Bourbon Association's tasting wheel.

The flavor wheel is simply a guide that helps you put words to what you're feeling in your mouth. The first few times you do a tasting exercise, it's important to just sip the bourbon and keep your mind open to what you're smelling and tasting. Start with the simple terms on the inner tier of the flavor wheel, like "sweet" or "spicy." As you get more experience tasting bourbon, you can work your way to the outside tiers, where the descriptors become more specific.

In the end, flavor or tasting wheels give drinkers the words to describe what they taste on their palate. And while this can sometimes veer off into a pretentious exercise in colorful vocabulary, being able to describe what you're experiencing can make you a more confident bourbon drinker.

In the American Bourbon Association's tasting wheel, there are five main flavor categories that drinkers can use as starting points: sweet, spice, grain, wood, and fruit/floral. These are top-line "notes" that are easy to identify.

Let's say that you take a sip of a bourbon and realize that it tastes of both fruit and spice. In consulting the wheel, you can determine whether the "fruit" flavor falls into one of these subcategories: cooked, dried, fresh, berry, or tropical. If it tastes of berry, for instance, you can then take another sip and nail down whether it's more akin to blackberry, raspberry, blueberry, or cherry.

Following the same procedure for "spice," you're faced with similar increasingly specific subcategories: aromatic and earthy. "Aromatic" includes flavors

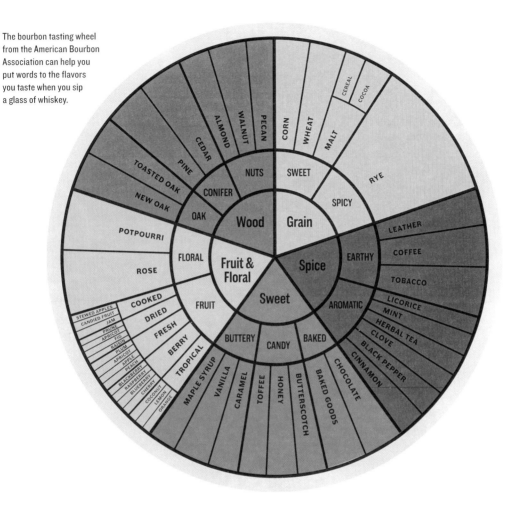

The bourbon tasting wheel from the American Bourbon Association can help you put words to the flavors you taste when you sip a glass of whiskey.

(and scents) like licorice, mint, herbal tea, clove, black pepper, and cinnamon; "earthy," meanwhile, refers to leather, coffee, and tobacco. A bourbon, of course, can have multiple notes from the same category, so this hypothetical bourbon could have notes of black pepper *and* coffee.

So, in the end, you could describe the bourbon as such: "It has strong notes of blackberry, black pepper, and coffee." The actual bourbon has never touched any of these fruits or spices, but your perception of these flavors is very real, and they make the bourbon experience more fulfilling. Once you start to home in on these flavors, you also gain a new respect for distilling as an art form. To be able to experience so many unique and varied flavors in a distilled spirit is truly something miraculous.

# THE IMPORTANCE OF A RICKHOUSE

The rickhouse (or rackhouse) is a rectangular structure designed to store bourbon barrels. This is where the aging happens, turning a clear distillate into a brown liquid infused with the flavors of charred oak. When you drive across the countryside of Kentucky, you'll see massive rickhouses dotting the landscape, huge buildings where bourbon barrels rest on their sides. Rickhouses are not temperature controlled, so they're vulnerable to the temperature fluctuations of the four seasons. This is by design—the changing temperatures allow the wood of the barrels to expand and contract, creating the distinctive color and flavor of bourbon.

The architecture of a rickhouse is intricate. The structure that holds the bourbon barrels rests on beams that do not rely on the exterior walls for support, so if the outer walls were to collapse, the interior structure would stay intact. Each row of barrels has a walkway alongside for airflow and to allow workers to inspect the barrels. Barrels age at different rates, depending on where they rest inside the rickhouse. The ones at the top are exposed to hotter temperatures, so evaporation happens faster than it does in the barrels lower to the ground. The barrels toward the windows will produce a bourbon that tastes different from the barrels in the middle. Barrels are far too heavy to rotate or move during the aging process, so once the barrels mature, it's time for the master distiller to step in. The job of the master distiller is to taste through the barrels and blend the different bourbons together to obtain a consistent flavor year after year. It is both a science and an art.

I like spending time in rickhouses. They are quiet and peaceful. There's usually a cat or two roaming the dusty halls looking for intruders. Cobwebs make their home in rickhouses. Sunshine beams through the open windows, creating dreamy shafts of light. Standing in a rickhouse means bathing in the aroma of tens of thousands of barrels of bourbon quietly aging and developing flavor.

# CENTRAL KENTUCKY

The region between the cities of Lexington and Louisville is generally referred to as Central Kentucky, but I like to think of it as a place touched by the gods of bourbon. The landscape is full of sun-kissed rolling hills, green pastures occupied by grazing horses, weathered barns, family-run farms, and the scent of bourbon carried everywhere by the gentle wind.

You can begin this tour from any direction, east or west, but I start from Louisville. Starting in Crestwood, visit **KENTUCKY ARTISAN DISTILLERY**, a contract distiller that makes, among other brands, the Jefferson's Bourbon line. Under the helm of Trey Zoeller, the brand has been experimenting with some of the most radical and groundbreaking ideas in bourbon finishes, like aging full barrels in the ocean over months to mimic the original journey of bourbon barrels traveling down the Mississippi (see page 154).

**BULLEIT DISTILLING CO.** is a short drive east and is the start of a grand bourbon tour that will wind you through some of Kentucky's powerhouse distilleries. A relative newcomer, Bulleit was one of the fastest-growing bourbons in the world, gracing the shelves of pretty much every bar and restaurant across the country. Just up the road in Shelbyville is **JEPTHA CREED DISTILLERY**; owned by the Nethery family, the distillery, farm, and historic Scottish lineage make for a natural connection between the land, the history, and the spirit that they bottle. **CASTLE**

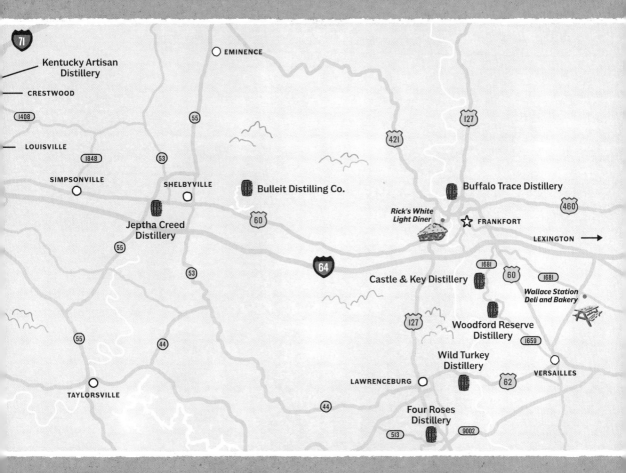

71

CRESTWOOD

1408

LOUISVILLE

EMINENCE

Kentucky Artisan
Distillery

55

53

127

421

1848

SIMPSONVILLE

SHELBYVILLE

Bulleit Distilling Co.

Buffalo Trace Distillery

460

Jeptha Creed
Distillery

60

Rick's White
Light Diner

FRANKFORT

LEXINGTON →

55

53

64

Castle & Key Distillery

1681

60

1681

Wallace Station
Deli and Bakery

127

Woodford Reserve
Distillery

1659

55

44

Wild Turkey
Distillery

VERSAILLES

LAWRENCEBURG

62

TAYLORSVILLE

44

Four Roses
Distillery

513

9002

**& KEY DISTILLERY** is the result of a project that reopened this famed distillery after years of disarray and neglect. The new owners kept the odd European architecture, and many of the original structures are still standing, making a distillery tour a unique experience where the ghosts of the past tread happily on the grounds of the present.

At this point, you'll want to grab a sandwich at Wallace Station Deli and Bakery. The pimiento cheese is some of the best you'll ever have, and don't forget to wash it all down with a local Ale-8-One soda.

The next distilleries on this tour are some of the most recognizable and historical brands and have formed the foundation of the bourbon industry behemoth that we know today. There are some names in bourbon history that command instant reverence, and Jim Rutledge is one of those. He's a master distiller and hometown hero whose success in reviving the **FOUR ROSES DISTILLERY** has provided a blueprint for everyone else in bourbon. (I won't spoil the story of how Paul Jones Jr. decided to name his bourbon Four Roses, but it's worth the visit to the distillery just to hear the charming story firsthand.)

The next stop is the famous **WILD TURKEY DISTILLERY** in Lawrenceburg. Wild Turkey may not be the most fashionable bourbon on the market today, but there wouldn't be a modern bourbon industry if not for Jimmy Russell, the longest-tenured master distiller in the world, whose career has spanned over sixty years. You would be insane not to think there is great wisdom in these bottles.

Many people would rightly argue that **WOODFORD RESERVE DISTILLERY** ignited the craft bourbon era when it introduced its namesake bourbon in 1996. At a time when bourbon was still mired in a low-reputation narrative, Woodford came out with a proud Kentucky mission statement, a unique bottle shape, and a dedication to make bourbon cool again. Under the watchful guidance of master distillers Chris Morris and Elizabeth McCall, the brand has succeeded beyond anyone's imagination. But with annual sales topping over a million cases a year, you can hardly refer to them as a craft distiller these days.

**BUFFALO TRACE DISTILLERY** makes some of the most sought-after bourbons in the world, including the labels George T. Stagg; Blanton's; W. L. Weller; Colonel E. H. Taylor, Jr.; and the impossible-to-find Pappy Van Winkle you've been dying to get your hands on. If you don't know the name of Harlen Wheatley, you should, because all this success has happened under his tenure—and if it seems like you're walking on hallowed ground here, that's because you are.

On your way out of town, be sure to stop in at Rick's White Light Diner in Frankfort to unwind with a burger and a beer while you take in the memorabilia from this part of Kentucky.

# MUSHROOM GRILLED CHEESE WITH BOURBON GRAVY

Mushrooms and their forest-floor flavor, which concentrates into deep, rich notes when cooked, highlight the umami-ness in bourbon. Provolone pairs wonderfully with mushrooms and bourbon. This is a decadent sandwich, and the addition of the Bourbon Onion Jam makes it unstoppable. The jam is listed as optional because I don't want you to skip this sandwich if you don't have the onion jam on hand. But try it one time, and you'll be convinced. The bourbon gravy on the side for dipping makes this sandwich even more decadent.

### Makes 2

5 tablespoons unsalted butter

I cup finely chopped onions

12 ounces cremini or button mushrooms, stemmed and finely chopped

¼ teaspoon kosher salt

Pinch of freshly ground black pepper

3 tablespoons bourbon

1½ teaspoons balsamic vinegar

1½ teaspoons soy sauce

½ teaspoon sugar

4 slices sourdough bread, about 6 inches long by 4 inches wide

2 teaspoons mayonnaise

8 slices provolone cheese

I tablespoon Bourbon Onion Jam (optional; page 67)

Bourbon Gravy (recipe follows), for serving

In a large skillet, melt 1 tablespoon of the butter over medium heat. Add the onions and cook, stirring often, for 3 minutes. Add 3 tablespoons butter to the skillet, then add the mushrooms, salt, and pepper. Increase the heat to high and cook the mushrooms, stirring continuously, for 5 minutes, until they've released their liquid and the liquid has almost entirely boiled off. Reduce the heat to medium-low and cook for 12 minutes more, until slightly browned; the skillet should be dry.

Stir in the bourbon, vinegar, soy sauce, and sugar. Cook, stirring frequently, until all the liquid has cooked off, about 6 minutes. Transfer the mushroom mixture to a bowl and set aside until you build the sandwiches.

« CONTINUED »

Lay the bread out on a cutting board. For each sandwich, spread a teaspoon of mayo on one slice of bread. Top both pieces of bread with 2 cheese slices each. Add about ¼ cup of the mushroom mix to one slice of bread. If using the bourbon onion jam, add a teaspoon or so over the mushrooms. Repeat to make a second sandwich.

Wipe out the skillet and heat it over medium heat. Add the remaining 1 tablespoon butter and let it melt. Add the sandwiches and cover with a lid. Cook for 2 minutes, then flip the sandwiches, cover, and cook for 3 minutes on the second side. Slice and serve right away, with a side of warm bourbon gravy.

# BOURBON GRAVY

You can use this all-purpose gravy with roasted chicken, your Thanksgiving turkey, meatloaf, or even hamburgers. But for the Mushroom Grilled Cheese (page 203), the best way to enjoy this gravy is to pour it into a cup, then dip the sandwich in the gravy with each bite.

### Makes 2½ cups

3 tablespoons unsalted butter

2 tablespoons all-purpose flour

2 cups beef stock

¼ cup bourbon

½ cup heavy cream

Kosher salt

In a large skillet, melt the butter over medium heat. Whisk in the flour and cook for 1 minute. Pour in the stock and bourbon and simmer for 5 minutes. Add the cream and cook for another 2 minutes, until thick and creamy. Season with salt and serve hot.

# BROWN RICE, SPELT, AND BOURBON RISOTTO

This soft rice-and-grain dish isn't a risotto in the traditional sense, but the slow-cooking technique is similar. The nutty, umami, and earthy flavors are warm and comforting. Make this dish on the first chilly night of autumn, when the leaves are brown and damp. Pair it with an aged bourbon on the rocks with a dash of your favorite bitters.

**Serves 2 as a main**

¼ cup brown rice

¼ teaspoon kosher salt

1½ teaspoons olive oil

½ onion, diced

2 garlic cloves, minced

6 ounces cremini mushrooms, chopped

1 cup spelt

¼ cup bourbon

4 cups vegetable stock

1 tablespoon unsalted butter

½ cup grated Parmesan cheese, plus a few bigger ribbons for serving

1 Bosc pear, diced

Freshly cracked black pepper

Pinch of Bourbon Salt (page 78)

In a small pot, combine ½ cup water, the rice, and the salt. Bring to a simmer over medium-high heat, then reduce the heat to low, cover, and simmer for 35 minutes, until the rice is tender and all the water has been absorbed.

In another pot, heat the olive oil over medium heat. Add the onion and garlic and let them sweat for 3 minutes. Add the mushrooms and cook for 3 minutes. Add the spelt and the bourbon. Cook until most of the alcohol has cooked off, about 4 minutes. Add 3 cups of the stock and simmer for 25 minutes, until the liquid has been absorbed and the spelt is tender yet still has a little chew to it.

Add the cooked rice and remaining 1 cup stock to the pot. Cook, stirring continuously, until the liquid has been almost completely absorbed. The risotto should not be clumpy. Add the butter and grated Parmesan. Cook until the risotto is creamy and tender and just barely holding its shape, about 4 minutes.

Transfer the risotto to warmed plates and top each serving with a few Parmesan ribbons. Garnish with the diced pear, cracked pepper, and bourbon salt. Serve right away.

# WHISKEY ONION SOUP

This recipe is inspired by the classic French onion soup recipe that I first made as a kid cooking from the legendary cookbook *Joy of Cooking*. Well, I'm not a kid anymore, and I don't live in France, so I flavor the soup with whiskey instead of wine.

**Serves 3**

3 pounds sweet onions, preferably Vidalia

8 tablespoons (1 stick) unsalted butter

1½ cups bourbon

⅓ cup pure maple syrup

⅓ cup soy sauce

2 tablespoons apple cider vinegar

4 cups beef stock

1 tablespoon kosher salt

Freshly ground black pepper

Cheddar Cheese Wafers (page 210), for serving (optional)

Slice the onions into thin strips, cutting from root to tip.

In a large pot or Dutch oven, melt the butter over medium heat. When the butter starts to foam, add the onions and increase the heat to medium-high. Cook, stirring regularly with a wooden spoon and making sure to mix from the bottom to the top, for about 10 minutes; the onions will release their moisture, then slowly start to caramelize on the bottom of the pot.

In a measuring cup, mix together the bourbon, maple syrup, soy sauce, and vinegar. When the onions have turned a golden brown, add a third of the bourbon mixture and scrape the bottom of the pot to release any browned bits. Cook until the liquid has evaporated and the onions begin to brown again. Repeat this process two more times. After the last addition of the bourbon mixture, let the onions cook for 2 minutes to remove the flavor of the alcohol, then add all the stock. Bring to a simmer over medium heat, then cook for 20 minutes, until the onions are soft and brown and the soup has thickened slightly.

Season with the salt and pepper to taste, then serve in deep bowls, each garnished with a cheddar cheese wafer, if desired.

**« CONTINUED »**

# CHEDDAR CHEESE WAFERS

A cheddar wafer gives onion soup the same crunch as a toasted baguette but with cheesy flavor. I like these wafers so much, I make them even without the soup, just to eat as a snack. Make sure to use good-quality cheddar and shred it yourself. Don't use preshredded cheese, as it will not melt correctly.

**Makes 6**

6 ounces sharp cheddar cheese

3 tablespoons unsalted butter, at room temperature

¾ cup all-purpose flour

Pinch of cayenne pepper

Kosher salt and freshly ground black pepper

Preheat the oven to 375°F.

Grate the cheese on the largest holes of a box grater. Transfer 4 ounces (two-thirds) of the grated cheese to a large bowl. Add the butter and stir until combined. Add the flour, cayenne, and salt and black pepper to taste.

Transfer the cheese mixture to a work surface. Knead until it forms a dough that holds together when you squeeze it with your fist. Portion the dough into 6 balls.

On a clean work surface, place one ball of dough on a piece of parchment paper and roll it out into a round 3 to 4 inches in diameter. Leave the edges rough. Transfer the round of dough to a sheet pan and repeat with the remaining dough.

Bake for 10 minutes. Top the wafers evenly with the remaining 2 ounces grated cheese. Bake for another 3 to 4 minutes, until the cheese is melty. Remove from the oven and use immediately as a garnish for the whiskey onion soup or store in an airtight container at room temperature for up to 2 days to enjoy as a snack.

# SLOW-GRILLED CHINESE EGGPLANT IN BOURBON MISO

It always amazes me how fluidly the flavors in bourbon match with essential flavors of Asian cuisine. Eggplant miso is as classic a dish as you will find in Japanese and Chinese cookery—but add bourbon to it, and it becomes almost a new dish with a fresh calling. It is not Asian or Southern, just a beautiful marriage of the two.

**Serves 2 as an appetizer**

2 Chinese eggplants

½ cup apple juice

3 tablespoons bourbon

2 tablespoons dark miso paste

1½ tablespoons soy sauce

1 tablespoon sugar

1 tablespoon grated fresh ginger

2 tablespoons plus 2 teaspoons toasted sesame oil

1 teaspoon rice vinegar

4 garlic cloves, minced

2 king oyster mushrooms, thinly sliced lengthwise

Kosher salt and freshly ground black pepper

1 serrano pepper, thinly sliced

1 teaspoon sesame seeds

Cut each eggplant in half. Score the flesh side of each half with a crosshatch pattern.

In a large bowl, combine the apple juice, ¼ cup water, the bourbon, miso, soy sauce, sugar, ginger, 2 teaspoons of the sesame oil, the vinegar, and the garlic. Whisk together.

In a large sauté pan, heat 1 tablespoon sesame oil over medium heat. Add the mushroom slices and cook for 2 minutes on each side. Season with salt and black pepper. Remove from the pan and set aside on a plate.

Add the remaining 1 tablespoon sesame oil to the pan, then add the eggplant halves, flesh-side down. Cook for 2 minutes, then add the miso mixture. Cover the pan and cook over medium heat for 8 minutes. Open the lid and check the eggplant;

it should be slightly soft to the touch. Flip the eggplant and cook, uncovered, for 2 minutes more, until the eggplant is tender and the miso mixture has caramelized to a golden brown.

Transfer the eggplant to a platter. Place the mushrooms over the eggplant and drizzle the miso pan sauce over the top. Garnish with the sliced serrano and sesame seeds. Serve right away.

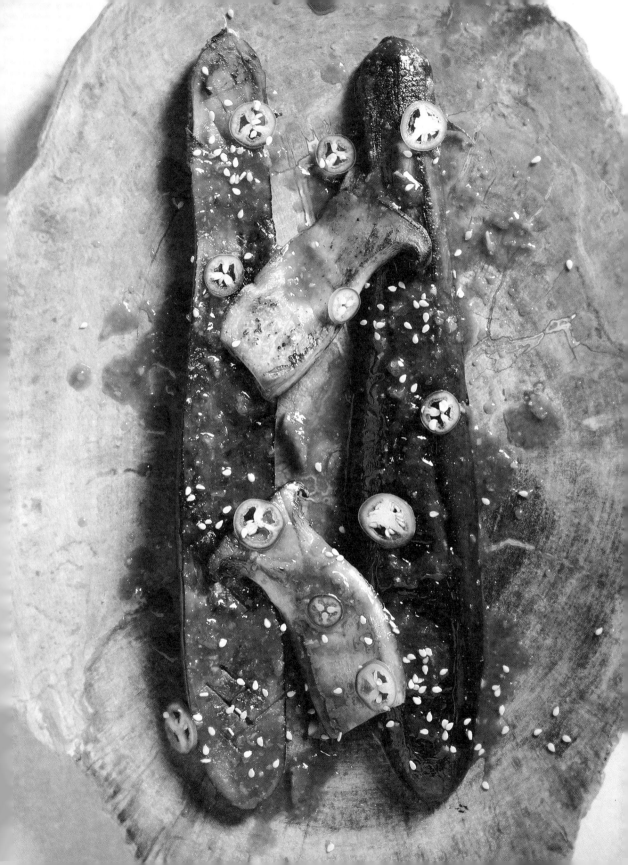

# POACHED OYSTERS
# IN BOURBON BROWN BUTTER

I like to use large East Coast or Gulf Coast oysters for this dish. But you don't need to worry about the region—just be sure to find fresh, large oysters that are plump and juicy. And when opening the oysters, make sure not to cut the oyster flesh with your oyster knife.

The grits should be so soft, they're borderline soupy. The oysters poach gently in the bourbon brown butter, which is warm and buttery but still feels alive in your mouth. The amount of the hot vinegar poured over the top is key—it should be a bit more than a dash but not enough to overpower the other flavors in the dish.

**Serves 2 as an appetizer**

2 cups chicken stock

½ cup stone-ground yellow grits

¼ cup bourbon

2 tablespoons unsalted butter

1 cup Bourbon Brown Butter
  (recipe follows)

10 oysters, shucked (see headnote)

Kosher salt

Chopped fresh chervil or parsley,
  for garnish

1 red Thai chile, thinly sliced

3 dashes of Hot Vinegar (recipe follows)

In a medium pot, combine 2 cups water and 1 cup of the stock. Bring to a boil over medium-high heat. While whisking continuously, slowly pour in the grits. Add the bourbon and cover the pot partially with a lid. Reduce the heat to medium-low and cook the grits, stirring occasionally, for 15 minutes. Uncover the pot and add the remaining 1 cup stock and the unsalted butter. Cook, stirring continuously, for 10 to 15 minutes, until the grits start to thicken. Reduce the heat to low and keep warm until ready to serve.

In a separate medium pot, warm the bourbon brown butter over medium heat, but don't let it simmer. The brown butter should be warm to the touch but not burning hot.

« CONTINUED »

Pat the oysters quickly with paper towels before adding them to the warm brown butter. Increase the heat to medium-high and cook the oysters for 45 seconds to 1 minute, depending on their size. When they're done, their edges should start to shrivel and their flesh will firm up, but they should still look plump and should still be raw and just warmed inside. Once the oysters are cooked, turn the heat off and use a slotted spoon to transfer them from the butter to a warm plate.

The warm grits may have thickened in the pot, so right before serving, add a few teaspoons of water to the pot and stir quickly. Spoon the grits onto a plate in a thin, flat layer. Top with the warmed oysters. Spoon some of the bourbon brown butter over the grits and oysters. Season with a little salt. Garnish with a little chervil or parsley and a few slices of Thai chile. Sprinkle the hot vinegar over the top and serve right away.

# HOT VINEGAR

A dash or two of this vinegar wakes up food with a spicy kick of acid. There's always a jar of this in my fridge, but it doesn't last very long, so my suggestion is to double the recipe.

**Makes 2 cups**

2 cups rice vinegar

3 red Thai chiles

2 star anise pods

1 jalapeño, sliced

1 knob (about 1 inch) fresh ginger, peeled

In a small pot, combine the vinegar, chiles, star anise, jalapeño, and ginger and bring to a boil over high heat. Boil for 1 minute, turn off the heat, and let cool for 5 minutes. Transfer the mixture to a lidded glass jar. Store in the fridge for up to 1 month.

# BOURBON BROWN BUTTER

One of bourbon's most sensual qualities is the nutty, caramelized aroma that comes from years of aging in an oak barrel. Browning has a similar effect on butter. Merging them together in a sauce is about as close to perfection as can be. Use this butter on dishes where you want a deep, nutty flavor that's also delicate, so think seafood—shrimp, clams, scallops.

**Makes about 1 cup**

12 tablespoons (1½ sticks) unsalted
    butter

1 teaspoon sea salt

½ cup bourbon

A few drops of fresh lemon juice

In a small pot, warm the butter over medium heat until it begins to foam, about 2 minutes. Add the salt and cook until the butter begins to turn brown and a nutty aroma wafts through the air, about 2 minutes more. Turn off the heat and scrape the bottom of the pot with a wooden spoon. Add the bourbon to the butter very slowly; it will bubble up violently. Stir in all the bourbon, add a few drops of lemon juice, and keep warm until ready to serve.

# BOURBON-POACHED BASS
# WITH PEAS AND SCALLIONS

Poaching fish in white wine is a classic technique for achieving buttery-soft, tender fish cradled in the flavors of the wine. The same technique can be used with bourbon. Because bourbon is much stronger than wine, your resulting broth will reflect the flavors in the bourbon. The results are phenomenal: a light, silky sauce with distinctive bourbon flavor whistling in the background. You will need fish bones for this broth; you can get them at any market that sells and portions whole fish.

**Serves 4 as a main**

I tablespoon olive oil

I onion, cut into wedges

I leek, cut into chunks and rinsed to remove grit

3 tablespoons garam masala

2 cups bourbon

I pound fish bones (see headnote), cut into small pieces

8 dried shiitake mushrooms

I lemon, cut in half

I (2-inch) square kombu

2 tablespoons soy sauce

½ teaspoon kosher salt, plus more as needed

4 (3- to 4-ounce) bass fillets

8 ounces soba noodles

I tablespoon white miso paste

I tablespoon unsalted butter

I½ cups frozen peas

3 scallions, thinly sliced

In a large pot, heat the olive oil over medium heat. Add the onion and leek and cook for 2 minutes to soften. Add the garam masala and stir. Add the bourbon and increase the heat to high. Cook to reduce the liquid by one-third, about 6 minutes.

Place the fish bones in the pot, then add 3 quarts water, the shiitakes, lemon, kombu, soy sauce, and salt. Bring to a boil, then reduce the heat to medium-low to maintain a very gentle simmer and cook for 45 minutes. Periodically skim off and discard any foam that comes to the top. Remove from the heat and strain the broth through a sieve (discard the solids). You'll have more broth than you need for this recipe, but it keeps well in an airtight container in the freezer for up to 2 months.

« CONTINUED »

In a high-sided pot that will fit all the fish, bring 8 cups of the broth to a light simmer over low heat.

Season the bass fillets with salt on both sides. Carefully add them to the broth. (The broth should register about 180°F on an instant-read thermometer, which is just below a simmer.) Gently cook the fish until opaque, 10 to 12 minutes, depending on the thickness of the fillets.

In a separate pot, cook the soba noodles according to the package instructions, usually about 10 minutes. Drain the noodles and divide them among four bowls. Carefully remove the fish fillets from the broth with a slotted spoon and place one fillet on top of the noodles in each bowl.

Return the broth to a boil and whisk in the miso and butter. Add the peas and cook for 1 minute. Taste and season with salt as needed. Spoon the broth and peas over the fish. Garnish with scallions and serve.

# BRAISED BEEF SHANKS IN BOURBON SAUCE

The flavors in bourbon do not fade during a long, gentle braise; they actually get deeper and more flavorful. Here the beef bathes in bourbon and transforms into a trembling, melty portion of bovine perfection. Turnips turn into something buttery and soulful. Pair this warming braise with a small glass of your best whiskey.

**Serves 2 as a main**

2 (I-pound) bone-in beef shanks

Kosher salt and freshly ground black pepper

I tablespoon olive oil

3 cups beef stock

¾ cup bourbon

I½ tablespoons soy sauce

I tablespoon Worcestershire sauce

I½ teaspoons balsamic vinegar

5 ounces pearl onions (about I0 onions), peeled (see Note)

4 baby carrots

I turnip, peeled and cut into wedges

2 tablespoons unsalted butter

Season the beef shanks with salt and pepper and let them rest for 15 minutes.

In a large pot, heat the olive oil over medium-high heat. Add the beef shanks and brown on all sides for 2 minutes. Add the stock, 2 cups water, and ½ cup of the bourbon. Reduce the heat to low and bring the liquid to a low simmer. Add the soy sauce, Worcestershire, and vinegar. Partially cover the pot with a lid and gently simmer the beef shanks for 2½ hours. Check periodically to make sure the liquid has not reduced to expose the beef shanks, and add more water to the pot so the beef shanks remain mostly submerged, if needed.

After 2½ hours, check the beef. It should be almost tender enough to fall off the bone at this point. Add the remaining ¼ cup bourbon, the pearl onions, carrots, and turnip. Cover the pot and simmer for 20 minutes more. Add the butter and simmer for 5 minutes more. Turn off the heat and let the beef rest, uncovered, for 10 minutes.

**« CONTINUED »**

Transfer the beef shanks to a plate and top with the vegetables and reduced braising liquid from the pot. Season with a little salt and pepper and serve immediately.

**NOTE**: To peel pearl onions, cut off the top and bottom of each onion and place them in a bowl with 2 tablespoons water. Cover with plastic wrap and microwave on high for 45 seconds. Drain the onions, then peel off their skins by rubbing them with a paper towel; the skins should come away easily. If you don't have a microwave, simmer the onions in a sauté pan with ¼ cup water for 2 minutes, then drain and use the same technique to peel them.

# COPPER AND CARAMEL

The first time I was tasked with making caramel from scratch, I was given a 5-pound bag of sugar, butter, some heavy cream, and no instructions. I burned it twice in an aluminum pan before one of the line cooks took pity on me and pointed to a copper rondeau hanging from a pot rack. Slowly melting and browning sugar into caramel is tricky work, and your pan has to be just the right temperature. You can't stir the sugar with a spoon, or it will seize up. You must gently swirl the pan until all the sugar melts into an amber pool. I learned all this before the chef returned to the kitchen to scowl at me. I learned the magic of a copper pan, how it can distribute heat evenly over a mound of sugar so you don't end up with blackened, smoking sugar on one side of your pan and unmelted sugar granules on the other. I started my love affair with copper pans that day, and I've been collecting them ever since, buying everything I can, from thrift store finds to E. Dehillerin saucepans.

Copper is a miracle metal, and it has been connected to the craft of cookery and distillation from its earliest records. Like yeast and bacteria, our relationship to copper was formed at a time before humans could explain how it chemically worked. Copper was the metal preferred for distillation for many reasons: First, copper is malleable. At a time in history when tools were rudimentary, copper was easy to hammer and shape into stills for distillation. Copper conducts heat quickly and evenly. This is convenient in cooking but essential in distilling. But probably the most important function of copper is its ability to eradicate certain types of bacteria and to control fungus. Copper is often used as an algicide for water purification. So many things contribute flavor in bourbon, but copper is important because of what it *removes* from the flavor profile of bourbon. Copper is a purifier of bourbon.

Vendome Copper & Brass Works is one of the world's leading copper still producers and is located in downtown Louisville, just a few blocks from the Ohio River and the city's car impound lot. You may not be familiar with the company's name, but if you've had your fair share of Kentucky bourbon, you've benefited from their expertise. If you tour the distilleries of Kentucky, the centerpiece of every tour is a beautiful copper pot still or column still: shiny, reflective, ancient, and modern at the same time. You can take a selfie in front of it, admiring the immense size of it, stretching to the ceiling. You can peek through a window in the copper to see the clear distillate sloshing around inside. (If you're lucky, you can taste a sip of that white dog and feel like it's burnt a hole through your esophagus.) And if you look closely at the plaque affixed to the side, you'll probably see the Vendome logo proudly displayed there.

According to Shawn Stevens, a retired Vendome metalworker, there's a long legacy of copper being used in manufacturing processes. "That's been the case for probably seventy-five hundred years," he explains. "Copper was probably used because it was malleable before anything was thought of with regards to what chemical properties it had. It was the Romans who figured out that copper was antibacterial. That's why they used it for their water pipes, their cooking utensils."

This is due to copper's physical structure. No matter how slick and polished its exterior looks to the human eye, if you toss a piece of copper under a microscope, it looks almost like a Brillo pad, with all the atoms in a gridlike alignment. The "larger, nastier atoms and molecules," Shawn says, "get trapped in the grid, while the lighter and fruity-flavored ones go up." Those nastier molecules are a group of chemical compounds in the sulfur family. They create the smells and flavors that can remind you of burnt matches, rotten eggs, and, yes, farts. These are qualities that we generally agree we don't want in our bourbon. Copper purifies and detoxifies.

Vendome's history is the history of American whiskey. The still family-owned business was founded by W. Elmore Sherman Sr. and is now overseen by a fourth generation of Shermans. When I toured Vendome with Rob Sherman, walking through the factory was like walking through an airport hangar filled with massive stills and fermenters in different stages of production. The sound of hammers banging on copper sounds both industrial and ancient. There were welders in certain rooms, and in others, large sheets of mirrorlike copper were just waiting to be bent and bolted into stills. There's a rhythm to the work, much like the relentless sounds of the cooperage. Shapes are created by trial and error. Know-how is passed on by repetition. There are no manuals for this kind of work; it is instinctual and tactile. Rob shows me an old still so oxidized, it's pitch-black. It was built in 1913 and shipped to Juárez, Mexico, where unscrupulous distillers used it to make whiskey that they illegally shipped back to the United States during Prohibition. Someone unearthed it, saw the Vendome logo, and called Rob to ask if he wanted it. He had it shipped back to Louisville and proudly displays it at the company's headquarters.

No one knows for sure when Vendome was founded, but the earliest Vendome still on record was produced in 1910. In the early days, Vendome did business with companies like E. H. Taylor, Jr. & Sons and J. T. S. Brown & Sons, who were reputable customers. Then Prohibition happened, and Vendome lost most of their customers overnight. They survived by working with companies that were able to produce medicinal alcohol and others that were making ethanol for fuel. When the Twenty-First Amendment repealed Prohibition in 1933, the distilling industry thrived, and demand for Vendome stills skyrocketed. In 1937, the Ohio River flooded and nearly collapsed their factory, which was located near the river.

After the boom of the 1930s, the constraints of World War II meant that by 1942, all distilleries were prohibited from producing beverage alcohol because of the demand for ethyl alcohol for wartime use. When the war ended, the public's taste for whiskey started to wane, and many of Vendome's longtime customers closed their businesses. This was a dark time for bourbon, but Vendome weathered the bust years, doing most of their business out of state and working with clients in the chemical, pharmaceutical, dairy, and confectionery industries. Then the craft distillery boom happened in the 1990s, and ever since then, Vendome has never been busier.

It may seem standard now to walk into a craft distillery and see a beautifully crafted copper still, shiny and glistening, as the centerpiece. But in the history of bourbon, this wasn't always the case. Bourbon's early days were rife with snake oil salesmen, shysters, and fraudulent producers. Distillers were making alcohol in backyard stills built from wood and whatever scrap metal they could afford. The quality was poor, and getting drunk was cheap. Bars were dens of iniquity and prostitution. Whiskey was perceived as a moral weakness, and societal problems such as homelessness and criminal behavior were blamed on the liquor. The temperance movement was formed as a direct response to early whiskey culture.

Today, a copper still represents quality, one of the reasons every distillery displays their still so proudly. We've come a long way from the early days of Jacob Spears and bourbon barrels slowly aging on a riverboat ride down the Mississippi. We've come to a point in history where the romantic stories of the past are packaged with the science and precision of corporate ingenuity. But in all that technology and innovation, there is still an invisible art to bourbon, a stalwart tradition passed on from generation to generation, from the barrels in a cooperage to a copper still carefully shaped for a future distillery. We sometimes get nostalgic for the bygone years of bourbon, pining for the simpler days, when bourbon was not the most sought-after liquor. But the truth is, those early days were hard and fraught with anxiety and fraud and bankruptcy and corruption. I have tasted some amazing bourbons from the 1950s and '60s, but those basement finds are rare. The truth of the matter is that the quality and depth and breadth of bourbon have never been better. The people in Kentucky have never been prouder. And the potential has never been greater.

Bourbon, for all its complexity, is at its heart a deep, vanilla-scented, indulgent libation. The vanilla and caramel and almond and toffee notes are a natural pairing with our collective sweet tooth. Bourbon itself is not a sweet drink, but its sweeter notes give us the perception that it is. It pairs well with sweet desserts because our palate is not inundated with sugar from the bourbon, allowing the dessert to shine. The desserts in this book (pages 244 to 268) were created with bourbon as a partner. Restraint is not needed in desserts. Indulgence is a virtue. Bourbon will add depth and complexity to any dessert because of its age. It goes well with cream and eggs and floury cakes. It will stand up to big flavors like chocolate and cherries and nuts. And what better way to finish dinner than by pairing a bourbon-centric dessert with an aged bourbon swirling in a glass with a single melty ice cube?

# POT STILL VS. COLUMN STILL

A still is any apparatus used to distill a liquid and turn it into alcohol. Two kinds of stills are most commonly used in bourbon distillation: the pot still and the column still. Pot stills are made of copper and consist of a kettle where a liquid is heated. The alcoholic compounds turn into a vapor and rise through a conical neck, separating from the nonalcoholic compounds. Once the vapor is cooled, it turns back into a liquid that has a higher concentration of alcohol in it. This clear distillate is what is referred to in bourbon making as the "white dog," and is now ready to be aged in barrels.

Pot stills can distill only one batch at a time, which means that after every distillation process, the still must be opened up, the spent mash must be removed, and the kettle must be cleaned before firing up the still again for the next batch. This is an arduous and time-consuming task.

In 1830, an Irishman named Aeneas Coffey patented his column still design, which became known as the Coffey still or continuous still. His invention was the culmination of the work of a long line of scientists and engineers who had developed various continuous still machines, including Jean-Baptiste Cellier-Blumenthal, who patented the first continuous column still in 1813, and Robert Klein, the Scotsman who innovated the original column still into a more complex device that utilized a series of interconnected pots and pistons. Column stills are composed of a series of plates. The liquid runs down through the plates or trays and is hit with steam that vaporizes the alcohol, and that vapor then travels back up through the plates. Each plate is slightly cooler than the one below it, and it takes a lot of plates to create a pure, distilled product. This new type of still allowed for continuous distilling, which meant more alcohol production and fewer delays for cleaning.

Today, the vast majority of the bourbon industry uses column stills or a hybrid still with a pot still at its base connected to a column still. Now, you may be asking, why would anyone use a pot still today? The answer is cost and space. Pot stills are considerably less expensive than column stills and take up much less room. Some modern column stills, like the one at Old Forester Distilling Co. in Louisville, can rise up to 44 feet tall. For small craft distillers or companies just starting out in the industry, this investment is too large to underwrite.

There is also the nostalgia and tradition of the pot still that holds importance to many a distiller. When I walk into a distillery and see a shiny copper pot still, I feel the connection to whiskey's historic roots in Scotland and Ireland. There is really nothing more beautiful than the oblong shape of a copper still with a conical neck connected to a lyne arm, resembling the curve of a swan's neck. In every distillery that uses one, it is the centerpiece of the building and a source of pride and artistry.

# PAPER PLANE

Felicia Corbett is a longtime Louisville bartender who defines what it means to be in hospitality: She's warm and friendly and able to curate every cocktail to be exactly what the customer wants. She introduced me to the Paper Plane when I was stuck on what I should drink, and it's become one of my favorite cocktails.

**Makes 1**

¾ ounce bourbon or rye

¾ ounce Amaro Nonino

¾ ounce fresh lemon juice

¾ ounce Aperol

1 lemon twist, for garnish

Pour the bourbon, amaro, lemon juice, and Aperol into a cocktail shaker with ice and mix vigorously. Strain into a coupe. Garnish with the lemon twist.

"There are many reasons why I fell in love with bourbon . . . the memory making, the ever-expanding education, but the main reason is that it doesn't have to be pretentious. There are so many great bourbons, and the fun part is tasting the gamut to find *your* bourbon and the path it leads you on."

**—FELICIA CORBETT**

# STARTING A
# BOURBON COLLECTION

Your bourbon collection depends on how much money you want to spend. Start by making yourself a realistic budget, then purchase what you like. Don't worry about getting the rare labels and the vintage stuff. Stock up on what you know you'll drink. These bottles will become the foundation of your collection. When you come across a limited-edition or single-barrel bottling for sale, buy more than one. You'll probably want to drink through one bottle right away and keep the other one for posterity.

Browse the internet. There are private auctions and sales all the time. These bottles won't be cheap, but they're out there if you look. Make sure to verify the authenticity of any bottle before purchasing from a faceless seller online. Fraud in the bourbon world is becoming increasingly common as bourbon's popularity grows.

Make friends with your local spirits shop owner and local restaurants that carry bourbon. It can't hurt to be nice to them and tell them of your interest; they might let you know when they get a highly sought-after bottle. Keep in mind that it isn't always the highest bidder who gets the rare bottle. The one thing retailers hate is when you buy a bottle from them and turn around and sell it on the secondary market. If you're a nice person and the retailer knows you're going to drink the bourbon rather than resell it, that can go a long way.

Visit distilleries. Many distilleries sell bottles in their retail shop that they don't sell out of state or that you wouldn't be able to find otherwise. This is a great way to find a cool bottle that no one else in your neighborhood will have. Get on distillery mailing lists. They'll alert you when they're releasing their rare bottlings. And, once again, it doesn't hurt to be nice to your tour guide when you visit. They just might be able to advise you of a small, out-of-the-way liquor shop that has some great deals.

Bourbon is meant to be drunk. I despise nothing more than an impressive collection of unopened bourbon bottles. Bourbon bottles are not museum pieces—they should be enjoyed and shared. So have fun with your collection. Don't get too obsessive, and don't spend more than you can afford. Bourbon can get very expensive, very fast, so don't ever lose sight of the fact that it's just a liquid that can, and should, be drunk in the span of a few festive hours with good friends.

# THE CEO

# VICTOR YARBROUGH

To be the first at anything takes a great deal of courage and vision. To be the first African American–owned bourbon distillery in an industry that has historically been almost exclusively white is groundbreaking. Victor Yarbrough is the cofounder of Victory Global LLC, along with his two brothers, and leads the day-to-day operations of Brough Brothers Distillery. After graduating from the University of Kentucky, he earned a position at Goldman Sachs in London. When he found himself both missing the bourbon back home and wanting to introduce his Kentucky heritage to Europeans, he began to import bourbon to the UK and English hard cider to the US. He's now working full-time in the spirits industry, breaking new ground and creating history.

**Q:** *What's your favorite way to drink bourbon?*

**A:** My favorite way to drink bourbon is with lemonade. The sweet and tangy profile of lemonade pairs perfectly with Brough Brothers' sweeter bourbon profile. You can level it up by muddling fruit like strawberries or blueberries.

**Q:** *Brough Brothers is the first Black-owned bourbon distillery. What is the significance of that to you?*

**A:** To lead the first Black-owned distillery in Kentucky is extremely important to our story. It represents not only our journey as brothers and businessmen but also the journey of African Americans in the distillery space. We have opened doors for other African Americans to enter the space, as well as given our youth an opportunity to see success outside of the normal success stories of entertainment and sports.

**Q:** *You spent some time in London. Do you think bourbon will ever be as popular as Scotch there?*

**A:** I spent ten years in London, which is where our company started. Through my time there, I've experienced and partnered with some of the best restaurants, retailers, and bars. I've seen the start of the bourbon boom happen, coinciding with the influx of American-themed restaurants. I believe that bourbon will gain the same popularity as Scotch in twenty years' time due to changes in demographics and the growing influence of American culture in the UK.

**Q:** *You could have started your bourbon distillery anywhere. Why in Louisville?*

**A:** It was important to start it in our hometown; it allows us to create jobs within our community and inspire our community. We also have the support of our family and friends, which is critical when breaking barriers. We wanted to make our city proud by making history as the first African American–owned distillery in Kentucky.

**Q:** *What does the future of bourbon look like to you?*

**A:** The future looks bright. Brough Brothers is carving a niche in the industry by reaching a broader demographic than traditional bourbon drinkers. The industry as a whole is putting billions of dollars into the production of bourbon to meet worldwide demand for the next fifty years.

# BOURBON IN POP CULTURE

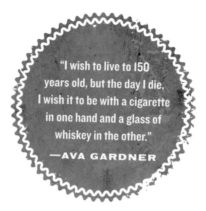

"I wish to live to 150 years old, but the day I die, I wish it to be with a cigarette in one hand and a glass of whiskey in the other."

—AVA GARDNER

Bourbon has had a long and contentious relationship with pop culture, and its characterization in television and film says a lot about our relationship to drinking culture.

In the classic Alfred Hitchcock thriller *North by Northwest*, Cary Grant plays Roger Thornhill, a Madison Avenue advertising executive who is kidnapped in a case of mistaken identity. While Thornhill is being held captive, two goons get him drunk on bourbon. Later, he calls his mother to explain what happened—the conversation goes like this: "These two men, they poured a whole bottle of bourbon into me. No, they didn't give me a chaser!"

Around the same time, Marilyn Monroe uses a hot-water bottle as a cocktail shaker to make a couple of late-night Manhattans in the 1959 hit movie *Some Like It Hot*. Bourbon in these days is a socialite's drink, and there's a familiarity and levity to it that makes it socially acceptable. But bourbon plays a darker role in the decades after, as it falls out of fashion in public perception.

In *The Hustler*, Paul Newman's "Fast Eddie" Felson is portrayed as a weak and flawed man who drinks bourbon as he hustles his way through seedy underground pool halls and gambling dens. During the climactic pool game, he drinks J. T. S. Brown bourbon straight from the bottle.

In the 1969 counterculture film *Easy Rider*, we witness Jack Nicholson (as George Hanson) drinking Jim Beam from a flask, and bourbon becomes associated with a culture tied to drugs and other criminal activities. In *The Shining*,

Roger Thornhill, played by Cary Grant (*center*), gets drunk on bourbon while held captive in the 1959 thriller *North by Northwest*.

the mentally unstable Jack Torrance (Nicholson again) orders bourbon at the hotel bar (though he is served Jack Daniel's).

The perception of bourbon reaches a sinister apex in the film *Blue Velvet*, when Frank Booth, a deranged criminal played by Dennis Hopper, drinks a bourbon right before he brutally rapes Isabella Rossellini's character, Dorothy Vallens. Bourbon has gone from a socialite's drink to a symbol of crime, weakness, and utter madness. This timing coincides with the bourbon industry losing out to the more popular spirits of the era, vodka and gin.

So what happened in the late 1990s to kick-start bourbon's renaissance? Yes, there was a renewed investment in luxury bourbon, and vodka had run its course with cotton-candy-flavored bottlings. But I believe two major contributing factors pushed bourbon over the edge. In the aftermath of the September 11 attacks, there was a newfound enthusiasm for all things American. Whether it was domestic craft cheese or the ingredients in our cocktails, chefs and bartenders were looking to fulfill the public's patriotic fervor for all things domestic. Russian vodka, British gin, and French wine were suddenly out of vogue. Bourbon is homegrown; it has history and tradition and a consistent flavor that makes it an ideal base for cocktails.

Also, around that same time, chefs and bartenders were drinking bourbon. It was cheap, and it was plentiful. In my early days working at restaurants, we would all get a shift drink or two after work. The owners wouldn't let the cooks order the Ketel One, but we could have all the Wild Turkey we wanted. Then chef and TV host Anthony Bourdain started to talk about bourbon and drink it on his shows. It's impossible to accurately measure the impact this one man had on the popularity of bourbon. All the chefs, bartenders, restaurant bloggers, and foodies were drinking it and adding to the obsession of getting your hands on a coveted bottle of Pappy Van Winkle. The world took notice, and so did Hollywood.

We see bourbon become sexy and cool in movies like *Crazy, Stupid, Love*. Bourbon becomes a status symbol in TV shows like *Silicon Valley* and *Succession*. It rises to iconic status in *Justified* and *Kingsman: The Golden Circle*. The perception of bourbon has come full circle. Bourbon is more popular than ever. This is a good thing. Bourbon deserves to enjoy this moment. And we can't talk about bourbon and pop culture and not include the ridiculous *Bob's Burgers* song "The Spirits of Christmas," with its endlessly repetitive refrain: "Oh, bourbon, bourbon, bourbon, bourbon . . ."

Jack Nicholson tries to order a bourbon in *The Shining*.

# NORTHERN KENTUCKY

The Ohio River borders Louisville and winds its way up north until it reaches Cincinnati. This important water route has connected Ohio and Kentucky via trade, commerce, and waterways throughout the history of the two states. Today, Northern Kentucky has a vibrant culture all its own that's part Cincinnati but still distinctly Kentucky, and the new wave of distilleries represents this.

If you're driving north on I-71, your first stop should be at the **NEELEY FAMILY DISTILLERY** in Sparta, a family-owned distillery that wears its moonshiner history proudly. Their unique distillery tour is a fascinating look at the connection between illegal and legal spirit distilling in Kentucky, and their vintage copper absinthe stills are amazing to see, so don't miss out on it. A little farther north is the **BOONE COUNTY DISTILLING CO.**, makers of fine bourbon and rye whiskey. The history of Boone County is on display here, and it proves that the connection between Cincinnati and Northern Kentucky and bourbon is a well-documented one and should be celebrated more.

As you inch closer to Cincinnati, stop at **SECOND SIGHT SPIRITS** for a quirky, new, and different approach to the distillery experience. Here you can taste bourbon or rum or buy tickets to a séance. It's a refreshingly fun take on bourbon as entertainment.

As the name suggests, **NEW RIFF DISTILLING** is a spirits brand that's going to forge a new path and take risks. While rooted firmly in the sour-mash bourbon tradition,

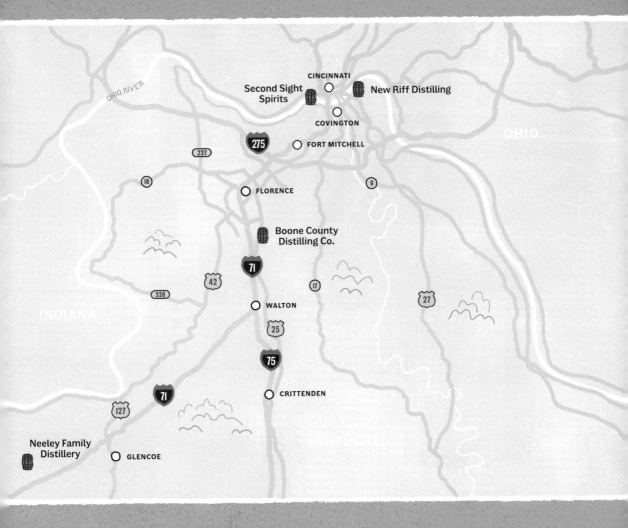

they're experimental in their grains and finishes, including high-rye recipes, heirloom grains, and malted wheats. The approach is proudly different and is exactly what's needed in bourbon today.

You're so close to Cincinnati; your best move is to spend the rest of the day taking in the culinary offerings of the Queen City. From Cincinnati chili, served over a bed of spaghetti and a mountain of finely shredded yellow cheese (trust me, you'll love it), to their local version of breakfast sausage called goetta to Graeter's ice cream, there's plenty to love about the city. Find any restaurant where Jose Salazar is cooking and you'll have a flawless meal, or if you want to explore every nook and cranny of Cincinnati's food scene, read articles by food writer Keith Pandolfi, who has uncovered every last culinary gem in this burgeoning city.

# BOURBON CHERRY ICE CREAM SANDWICHES

These cherry ice cream sandwiches are the cutest ice cream sandwiches you'll ever make. The ice cream is made in a mixer and chilled in a mold so no ice cream machine is needed, though it will take a day to freeze properly. The sandwich part is made with piecrust squares. It takes a little extra work to make the lattice-weave tops for the sandwiches, but the result is worth the effort.

**Makes 6 small ice cream sandwiches**

### FOR THE BOURBON CHERRIES

I cup whole cherries, pitted and sliced into 4 pieces each

I tablespoon sugar

¼ teaspoon kosher salt

2 tablespoons unsalted butter

2 tablespoons bourbon

### FOR THE CRÈME FRAÎCHE ICE CREAM

I cup heavy cream

I teaspoon pure vanilla extract

2 tablespoons sugar

¼ teaspoon kosher salt

I (14-ounce) can sweetened condensed milk

I cup crème fraîche

### FOR THE PIE DOUGH

1¼ cups all-purpose flour, plus more for dusting

I teaspoon kosher salt

8 tablespoons (I stick) unsalted butter, cut into small pieces and chilled

2 large egg yolks

2 teaspoons whole milk

Line a 9-inch square baking pan with plastic wrap, enough to cover the bottom and sides of the pan.

To make the bourbon cherries, in a medium bowl, combine the cherries, sugar, and salt and toss to coat and combine.

In a shallow sauté pan, melt the butter over medium heat. When it starts to foam, add the cherries and sauté for about a minute. Add the bourbon and cook for 2 minutes more. Remove from the heat and let cool for 10 minutes, then drain off the liquid and reserve it for the ice cream. Set the cherries aside.

To make the crème fraîche ice cream, in the bowl of a stand mixer fitted with the whisk attachment or in a large bowl using a handheld mixer, combine the heavy cream, vanilla, sugar, salt, and 1 tablespoon of the reserved cherry liquid and whip on medium speed until stiff peaks form, about 3 minutes. Reduce the mixer speed to low and stream in the condensed milk. By hand, use a spatula to fold in the crème fraîche until combined.

Spread half the ice cream batter evenly in the prepared baking pan. Sprinkle the cooled bourbon cherries on top and cover with the remaining ice cream batter. Cover with a layer of plastic wrap pressed lightly against the top of the batter. Freeze overnight.

The next day, make the pie dough: In a medium bowl, combine the flour and salt. Add the butter and use your fingers to work it into the flour, until only pea-size chunks remain.

In another bowl, whisk together 1 egg yolk and the milk. Add the egg mixture to the bowl with the flour mixture and mix with your fingers until just combined.

Transfer the dough to a floured work surface and flatten it with your hands. Place the dough between two sheets of parchment paper, then roll it with a wooden rolling pin to $1/4$ inch thick. Transfer the dough on the parchment to a sheet pan and chill in the fridge until the dough is firm to the touch, about 15 minutes.

Preheat the oven to 350°F. Line a sheet pan with parchment.

Remove the dough from the fridge and transfer it to a work surface, still on the parchment. Cut the dough into twelve $2^{1}/_{2}$-inch squares. Place 6 squares on the prepared sheet pan; these are for the ice cream sandwich bottoms.

Use the remaining squares to make lattice-weave tops for the sandwiches: Place one of the remaining squares on a work surface and cut it into 7 even strips. Lay out 3 strips parallel to each other and slightly spaced apart. Fold back the middle strip. Now start weaving in the perpendicular strips. Place the first one perpendicular to the parallel strips, starting from the bottom. Unfold the folded strip so it lies over the perpendicular strip. Now take the parallel strips running underneath the perpendicular strip and fold them back. Lay down another perpendicular strip next to the first perpendicular strip. Unfold the folded parallel strips so they lie over the second perpendicular strip. Repeat with the remaining two perpendicular strips. When you're finished, you should have a lattice-weave pattern measuring 2½ inches square. Using a sharp knife, trim the edges to make them neat and square. Place the lattice square on the prepared sheet pan and repeat with the 5 remaining dough squares.

Transfer the sheet pan to the fridge and chill the dough for 15 minutes.

In a small bowl, whisk together the remaining egg yolk and 2 teaspoons water to make an egg wash. Remove the dough from the fridge and brush the squares evenly with the egg wash. Immediately transfer them to the oven. Bake for 10 to 12 minutes, until golden brown. Let cool to room temperature.

If you're not serving the ice cream sandwiches right away, store the piecrust pieces in an airtight container at room temperature until ready to use.

When you're ready to serve, remove the ice cream from the freezer. Unmold it from the pan by pulling the plastic wrap. (If it's stuck, you can invert the pan and run it under a little warm water to loosen it, but keep your hand under the pan in case the ice cream falls out.) Remove the plastic wrap from the ice cream carefully so as not to tear it, or the plastic might stick to the ice cream.

Cut the ice cream into 2½-inch squares. Use one of the piecrust bottoms as a reference to make sure the ice cream and the piecrusts are the same size.

Place the piecrust bottoms on a plate, top each with an ice cream square, and then finish each with a lattice-crust top. Serve right away or wrap in plastic wrap and freeze for an hour or two. Any leftover sandwiches should be wrapped and stored in the freezer for up to 1 week.

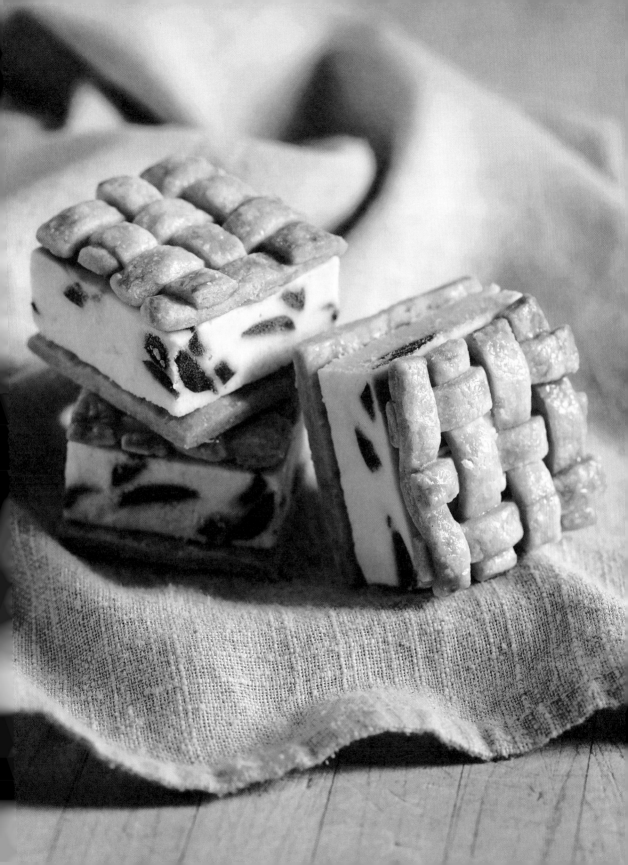

# BREAD CRUMB PANCAKES WITH BOURBON MAPLE SYRUP

This recipe was inspired by one I found in a vintage Kentucky cookbook from a time when resources were scarce and bread crumbs were cheaper than flour. We may not need to be so frugal anymore, but I love the texture of bread crumb pancakes. They are hearty with bite and bounce and chew. Top the pancakes with addictive Date-Bourbon Butter and simple but dreamy Bourbon Maple Syrup.

**Makes 16 pancakes**

1½ cups panko bread crumbs

3 cups whole milk

½ cup all-purpose flour

2 tablespoons sugar

1 tablespoon baking powder

1 teaspoon kosher salt

1 large egg, beaten

1 tablespoon unsalted butter, melted

Date-Bourbon Butter (recipe follows), for serving

Bourbon Maple Syrup (recipe follows), for serving

Place the panko in a large bowl. In a small pot, heat the milk over medium heat just until bubbles start to form around the edge of the pan. Pour the hot milk over the panko and whisk to combine, then let soak for 10 minutes.

In a separate bowl, combine the flour, sugar, baking powder, and salt. Add the flour mixture to the panko mixture, along with the egg and melted butter. Whisk thoroughly to remove any lumps.

Heat a large cast-iron skillet over medium heat. For each pancake, pour ¼ cup of the batter into the skillet and cook until the bottom is golden brown and the edges look dry, then flip and cook on the second side for 30 seconds. Transfer to a plate and repeat with the remaining batter.

Serve the pancakes warm, with date-bourbon butter and bourbon maple syrup.

« CONTINUED »

## DATE-BOURBON BUTTER

Date butter melts seductively on top of warm pancakes, but it's just as good on cinnamon toast or on a warm croissant in the morning. Use Turkish dates, if you can find them.

### Makes ½ cup

6 tablespoons (¾ stick) unsalted butter,
    at room temperature

2 dates, pitted and finely chopped

½ cup bourbon, reduced to
    2 tablespoons (see page 75)

I teaspoon honey

Pinch of kosher salt

In a small bowl, combine the butter, dates, reduced bourbon, honey, and salt. Store in an airtight container in the fridge for up to 3 weeks. Bring to room temperature before serving.

## BOURBON MAPLE SYRUP

Use the best-quality maple syrup you can find for this—it makes all the difference.

### Makes ¾ cup

¾ cup pure maple syrup

2 tablespoons bourbon

Pinch of kosher salt

In a small bowl, combine the maple syrup, bourbon, and salt. Store in an airtight container in the fridge for up to 1 month.

# BOURBON BALLS
## WITH TOFFEE-POPPED SORGHUM, MILK CHOCOLATE, AND BOURBON PECANS

Bourbon balls are a classic treat that's ubiquitous in Kentucky. Making them takes some effort, but the result is out of this world. Texturally layered and complex, bourbon balls can be served in place of a traditional dessert. Or treat them as an accompaniment to a bowl of vanilla ice cream.

**Makes about 12 bourbon balls**

**FOR THE BOURBON PECANS**

1 cup chopped pecans

½ cup bourbon

**FOR THE TOFFEE-POPPED SORGHUM**

¼ cup brown sugar

4 tablespoons (½ stick) unsalted butter

1 tablespoon corn syrup

1 cup popped sorghum (see Note; or substitute crushed popcorn)

Sea salt

**FOR THE BOURBON BALLS**

8 tablespoons (1 stick) unsalted butter, at room temperature

½ cup Brown Butter Bourbon Caramel Sauce (page 267)

3 cups confectioners' sugar

2 tablespoons bourbon

½ cup milk chocolate chips

1 cup unsweetened cocoa powder

To make the bourbon pecans, place the chopped pecans in a jar and add the bourbon. Add water, if needed, to completely submerge the pecans. Soak overnight, uncovered.

The next day, preheat the oven to 350°F. Line a sheet pan with parchment paper.

Drain the pecans and pat dry with paper towels. Spread them evenly over the prepared sheet pan. Bake for 10 minutes, or until dry and aromatic.

Line a second sheet pan with a clean sheet of parchment.

« CONTINUED »

To make the toffee-popped sorghum, in a small pot, combine the brown sugar, butter, and corn syrup and bring to a boil over medium heat. Cook, stirring occasionally to avoid burning, for 2 minutes. Fold the popped sorghum into the brown sugar mixture, then spread it evenly over the prepared sheet pan. Sprinkle the top with salt. Let cool for 10 minutes, then chop into small pieces similar in size to the pecan pieces.

To make the bourbon balls, in the bowl of a stand mixer fitted with the whisk attachment or in a medium bowl using a handheld mixer, combine the butter, bourbon caramel sauce, and confectioners' sugar and whip on medium-high speed until light and fluffy, at least 6 minutes. Add the bourbon and mix until combined. Add 1 cup of the bourbon pecans, 1 cup of the chopped popped sorghum, and the chocolate chips. Use a rubber spatula to mix by hand until thoroughly combined.

Form the dough into balls slightly smaller than a golf ball. Place them on a sheet pan and store, uncovered, at room temperature until ready to serve.

Just before serving, pour the cocoa powder into a small bowl. Roll the bourbon balls in the cocoa powder to coat, then serve right away.

**NOTE:** Whole-grain sorghum pops just like popcorn. You can buy sorghum easily on the internet; Bob's Red Mill carries it. Make sure not to purchase sorghum flour or sorghum syrup for this recipe; it's the whole-grain sorghum you are looking for. To pop sorghum, heat a sauté pan with a tight-fitting lid over high heat, then add the sorghum and a little vegetable oil and cover. As soon as you hear the sorghum beginning to pop, start shaking the pan vigorously. It will burn fast, so keep a watchful eye on it. If you can't get ahold of whole-grain sorghum, it's fine to use popcorn in this recipe; just crush it a bit to break it down into smaller pieces.

# FIG, WALNUT, AND SAFFRON KULFI
# WITH BOURBON HONEY

Kulfi, a frozen dessert made from sweetened and flavored milk, dates back to the sixteenth century. Though it's often described as Indian ice cream, it's not really ice cream at all. Kulfi is denser and richer and melts slower. It comes in all shapes and sizes; I use a muffin tin for this recipe. The saffron adds a bright color that makes this one of the prettiest desserts you'll ever see. If fresh figs are in season, you can use them instead of the dried figs; this dessert will work with either.

**Makes 18 kulfi**

### FOR THE BOURBON HONEY
3 tablespoons bourbon, reduced to 1½ tablespoons (see page 75)

6 tablespoons honey

### FOR THE KULFI
12 dried figs (see Note)

¼ cup bourbon

¼ cup sugar

6 ounces fresh raspberries

1 cup half-and-half

½ teaspoon saffron threads

1 cup heavy cream

1 (14-ounce) can sweetened condensed milk

1 teaspoon pure vanilla extract

¼ teaspoon kosher salt

To make the bourbon honey, pour the bourbon into a small pot and add the honey. Bring to a simmer over high heat and whisk together. Cook for 3 minutes, then let cool to room temperature. Transfer to a jar.

To make the kulfi, place the figs in another clean jar.

In a small pot, combine 1 cup water, the bourbon, and the sugar and bring to a boil over high heat. Boil for 2 minutes, then remove from the heat. Pour the bourbon water over the figs in the jar and let soak until rehydrated and cooled, about 15 minutes. Remove the figs from the water. Cut off and discard the stems, and slice the figs into quarters. Set aside.

**« CONTINUED »**

Cut the raspberries in half and set aside.

Line each compartment of an 18-cup muffin tin with plastic wrap.

Place most of the figs in the bottom and around the sides of the muffin tin compartments. Place most of the raspberries on the bottom and around the sides, too. Save some figs and raspberries to garnish the dessert later.

In a small pot, warm the half-and-half and saffron over medium heat until simmering. Immediately remove from the heat and transfer to a jar. Chill in the fridge, uncovered, for 1 hour.

Meanwhile, in the bowl of a stand mixer fitted with the whisk attachment or in a large bowl using a handheld mixer, whip the heavy cream on medium speed until it forms soft peaks, about 2 minutes. Reduce the mixer speed to low and stream in the condensed milk, vanilla, and salt. Stream in the chilled saffron half-and-half.

Pour the saffron kulfi over the figs in the muffin tin and freeze overnight, uncovered.

When you're ready to serve the dessert, remove the kulfi from the freezer and let it rest at room temperature for about 10 minutes. Unmold the kulfi from the muffin tin and carefully remove the plastic wrap, making sure not to tear it. Flip each kulfi over onto a plate or into a small bowl. Garnish the top with a fresh raspberry and a slice of fig. Drizzle the bourbon honey generously over the top and serve right away.

**NOTE**: There's a short season from summer to fall when you can find fresh figs. If you have them, you can swap them out for the dried figs in this recipe. If using fresh figs, cut them in half. Mix the bourbon and sugar together (omit the water) and let the fresh figs soak in the bourbon for a few minutes (no need to heat them). Drain the figs and continue with the recipe.

# LANE CAKE

I'm a vintage cookbook collector and I love recipes that come from a long-forgotten time. This cake originated in Alabama and is one of these delicious cakes that should be on everyone's menu but somehow got lost to the dusty pages of history. I've updated the recipe to be a bit more streamlined, but the core flavors are the same as the original. It's a showstopper of a cake, so make it for a special occasion.

**Serves 8 to 10**

### FOR THE CAKE

Nonstick pan spray

1 cup (2 sticks) unsalted butter, at room temperature

1 cup sugar

4 large eggs, separated

1 teaspoon pure vanilla extract

1½ cups all-purpose flour

1¾ teaspoons baking powder

1 teaspoon kosher salt

½ cup buttermilk

### FOR THE FILLING

2 cups half-and-half

1 teaspoon pure vanilla extract

8 large egg yolks

1¼ cups sugar

2 tablespoons cornstarch

¼ teaspoon kosher salt

1 cup chopped pecans, toasted

1 cup raisins, soaked in 1 cup bourbon overnight and drained

Zest of 1 orange

### FOR THE BOURBON BUTTERCREAM

6 large egg whites

1½ cups sugar

2 cups (4 sticks) unsalted butter, at room temperature

2 tablespoons bourbon

### FOR THE GARNISH

A few edible flowers

½ cup Candied Pecans (recipe follows)

Zest of 1 orange

To make the cake, preheat the oven to 350°F. Spray three 6-inch round cake pans with pan spray and line the bottoms with parchment paper cut to fit.

In the bowl of a stand mixer fitted with the paddle attachment or in a large bowl using a handheld mixer, cream the butter and sugar on medium-high speed until white and fluffy, about 5 minutes. Scrape down the sides of the bowl with a spatula.

« CONTINUED »

Reduce the mixer speed to low and add the egg yolks one at a time, then add the vanilla. Scrape down the sides again and mix until smooth.

In a separate bowl, combine the flour, baking powder, and salt. Add about half the dry mixture to the wet mixture and mix on medium speed to combine. Add about half the buttermilk to the batter and mix until incorporated. Add the remaining dry ingredients and buttermilk to the batter and mix again. When everything is incorporated, transfer the batter to another large bowl.

Clean out the mixer bowl (and the beaters, if using a handheld mixer) and put the egg whites in the bowl. If using a stand mixer, fit it with the whisk attachment. Whip on medium-high speed until medium peaks form, about 4 minutes. Fold the egg whites into the batter.

Distribute the batter evenly among the prepared pans and bake until golden and springy to the touch, 25 to 30 minutes. Remove the pans from the oven and let rest for 5 minutes on a sheet pan. Unmold the cakes from the pans, remove the parchment, and let the cakes rest and cool on the sheet pan for at least 30 minutes before filling and frosting.

To make the filling, in a medium pot, combine the half-and-half and vanilla and bring to a simmer over medium heat.

In the bowl of a stand mixer fitted with the whisk attachment or in a large bowl using a handheld mixer, combine the egg yolks, sugar, cornstarch, and salt and whip on medium-high speed until pale yellow and fluffy, about 3 minutes. Turn off the mixer and add 1 cup of the warm half-and-half mixture to the egg mixture. Stir well, then transfer the contents of the mixer bowl to the pot with the rest of the half-and-half mixture. Warm this mixture over medium heat, stirring continuously, until thickened, about 5 minutes. Remove from the heat and fold in the pecans, raisins, and orange zest. Let cool to room temperature.

To make the bourbon buttercream, fill a medium pot with a little water and bring to a gentle simmer over medium heat. Combine the egg whites and sugar in a heatproof bowl. Place the bowl directly over the simmering water (the bottom of the bowl should not touch the water) and cook, without stirring, until the sugar has dissolved and the mixture is warm. Transfer the mixture to the bowl of a stand mixer fitted with the whisk attachment and whip on high speed until a stiff white meringue develops, 3 to 4 minutes.

With the mixer running on low speed, slowly add small amounts of the softened butter and mix until incorporated. Add the bourbon and mix on medium speed until a smooth buttercream forms. If the mixture looks separated, your butter was too cold; just mix for a little longer until it warms up. If your buttercream is smooth but not thick, the mixture is too warm; cool it in the fridge for a few minutes and then whip again. Transfer the buttercream to a piping bag fitted with a round tip.

To assemble the cake, cut each cooled cake in half horizontally, creating 6 layers. You'll be using only 5 layers, so if one of the layers isn't perfect, you can discard it (or save it for a snack). Place the first layer on a cake plate. Pipe a thin layer of buttercream over the cake and spread it evenly with an offset spatula. Pipe more buttercream around the edge of the cake, leaving a 3-inch-diameter well in the center. Scoop enough filling into the well to fill it about three-quarters of the way to the top. Place another layer of cake over the filling and repeat this process until you have a 5-layer cake with 4 layers of filling and buttercream. Finish the top with a thin layer of buttercream and smooth it flat using an offset spatula.

Cover the sides of the cake evenly in buttercream. Using the back of a wet spoon, gently press into the buttercream at the base of the cake and drag upward to create decorative vertical stripes. Do not press too hard or you will remove the buttercream. Transfer any remaining buttercream to a second piping bag fitted with a star tip. Decorate the top with a few mounds of buttercream, then garnish with flower petals, a handful of candied pecans, and fresh orange zest. Store covered at room temperature for up to 3 days.

# CANDIED PECANS

Candied pecans are always in my pantry. They can be used as decoration on a cake, served with a cheese tray, or sprinkled on top of a bowl of ice cream. They also make a great midnight snack.

**Makes 1 cup**

1 cup pecan halves

2 tablespoons brown sugar

⅓ teaspoon kosher salt

Preheat the oven to 325°F. Line a sheet pan with parchment paper.

Place the pecans on a sheet pan and toast in the oven for 7 minutes. Let cool.

In a small pot, combine 2 tablespoons water, the brown sugar, and salt, and bring to a boil over high heat. Add the pecans and reduce the heat to low. Cook, stirring continuously, for 1 minute. Use a spider to strain out the pecans and transfer them to the prepared sheet pan in an even layer. Let the pecans cool and harden, about 20 minutes. Transfer to an airtight container with a lid. They should keep at room temperature for up to a week.

# THE LEGEND

# FRED NOE

Frederick "Fred" Booker Noe III is the son of the late Frederick "Booker" Noe Jr. and a great-grandson of Jim Beam. He's a seventh-generation distiller and became the master distiller for Jim Beam brands in 2007. He was born in 1954 in Bardstown, Kentucky, and grew up in the same house that the legendary Jim Beam once lived in. After graduating from Bellarmine University in Louisville, Fred joined the Jim Beam company and learned every aspect of the bourbon industry. Eventually, he played a crucial role in developing and promoting a line of premium bourbons and now serves as the ambassador of the Small Batch Bourbon Collection, a game changer in the world of bourbon. He's a living treasure and someone whose presence and character you won't soon forget if you happen to be in a room with him. Fred Noe was inducted into the Kentucky Bourbon Hall of Fame in 2013.

**Q:** *Do you drink bourbon, and if so, how do you drink it?*

**A:** I still enjoy a bourbon every now and then with a cube or two of ice and a little water.

**Q:** *Have bourbon tastes changed over the years?*

**A:** If you look back forty years ago, there weren't that many bourbons. We only had five products at Jim Beam at the time. But over time, people have become more educated, and they want more choices. Back then age statements weren't popular, but now consumers want to know what's in their glass. They like the stories behind the brands. They want more variety.

**Q:** *Did you always know you were going to be in the family business?*

**A:** When I was young, Dad actually tried to steer me away from the business because bourbon was not doing all that great at the time. He told me many times, "Don't bank on us even being here when you get older." A lot of distilleries went bankrupt in his generation. So I went to college and then I started as the night shift bottling line supervisor. I learned the whole industry from the bottom up.

**Q:** *How important is it to have a generational bourbon company?*

**A:** There's a lot of on-the-job training and generational knowledge. There are things that were passed down, and those learnings are valuable in continuing to run our business. We've been here for 225 years, so our learning curve is pretty good. We know the temperature, the climate, the water, and everything else from this region where we make bourbon. Right now, I'm the keeper of that knowledge, and I will pass it down to the next generation. My son, Freddie, is now working alongside me to take the business forward. I don't put any pressure on the kids to do this job, but once it's in your heart, then it's gotta be all in.

**Q:** *Do you remember Jim Beam?*

**A:** I was lucky enough to live in his house in Bardstown, Kentucky. But I was too young to remember the man. A lot of what we know about Jim Beam is from the stories from our grandmothers. He was a straightforward man, and he would not have approved of embroidering the truth. Every day, he wore a three-piece suit. He thought it was the proper way to present himself. We even have a picture of him fishing in a boat in Canada in a three-piece suit. He also enjoyed telling stories. No matter what, at 6:00 p.m., the family gathered around and told stories of their day with a glass of bourbon.

# BOURBON AND BUTTERSCOTCH PUDDING

So many flavors play well with bourbon, especially when it comes to desserts. Butterscotch is one that you might not immediately think of, but bourbon and butterscotch dance together with ease and grace. This is a simple and satisfying dessert. Fancy garnishes can complement the pudding, but you can also eat the pudding on its own, in a room, by yourself, and nothing else is needed.

**Serves 4**

4 tablespoons (½ stick) unsalted butter

I cup dark brown sugar

I cup half-and-half

2 cups whole milk

2 tablespoons bourbon

2 teaspoons kosher salt

I teaspoon pure vanilla extract

3 large egg yolks

¼ cup granulated sugar

3 tablespoons cornstarch

I0 grapes, thinly sliced

½ cup popped sorghum (see page 25I; or substitute crushed popcorn)

Almond Tuiles (recipe follows), for serving (optional)

In a medium pot, combine the butter and brown sugar and cook over medium heat until the butter melts and the sugar has dissolved. Reduce the heat to low and cook, stirring occasionally, for about 2 minutes.

Add the half-and-half, raise the heat to high, and bring to a boil. Turn off the heat and add the milk, bourbon, salt, and vanilla. Mix well and reduce the heat to its lowest setting to keep the butterscotch cream warm.

In the bowl of a stand mixer fitted with the whisk attachment or in a large bowl using a handheld mixer, combine the egg yolks, granulated sugar, and cornstarch and whip on high speed until pale yellow and fluffy, about 3 minutes. Reduce the mixer speed to low and add 1 cup of the warm butterscotch cream. Mix well, then slowly pour the contents of the mixer bowl into the pot with the remaining butterscotch cream. Cook over medium heat, stirring continuously, until the mixture thickens and bubbles start to pop up at the edges of the pot, 3 to 5 minutes.

« CONTINUED »

Pour the pudding mixture into a glass bowl and cover with plastic wrap pressed directly against the surface to prevent a skin from forming. Refrigerate until completely chilled, about 4 hours.

Meanwhile, arrange the grape slices in an even layer on a plate and freeze for 2 hours.

When ready to serve, remove the pudding from the fridge and remove the plastic wrap. Give the pudding a final mix with a spoon. Spoon the pudding into individual bowls and top with the frozen grape slices. Sprinkle the top with popped sorghum. Place a tuile in the middle, if desired, and serve right away.

## ALMOND TUILES

Almond tuiles are delicate in texture and temperamental to make. But they are worth the effort. Be patient with the process, and the tuiles will turn out just fine.

**Makes 4**

1½ cups sliced almonds

1 tablespoon all-purpose flour

Zest of ½ orange

Pinch of kosher salt

⅓ cup sugar

2 tablespoons unsalted butter

1 tablespoon heavy cream

1 tablespoon corn syrup

Preheat the oven to 325°F. Line a sheet pan with parchment paper.

Chop the almonds as finely as you can. Transfer them to a medium bowl and add the flour, orange zest, and salt.

In a small pot, combine the sugar, butter, cream, and corn syrup. Bring to a boil over high heat and stir to combine. Add the sugar mixture to the flour mixture and mix well. Let cool completely.

Spoon ½ teaspoon of the batter onto the prepared sheet pan for each tuile. Bake for 2 minutes, then rotate the pan and bake for 2 to 3 minutes more, until the tuiles are golden brown. Remove from the oven and gently slide the parchment from the pan onto a cool surface. Let the tuiles cool completely, then gently peel them from the parchment. Store in an airtight container at room temperature for up to 2 days.

# CORN ICE CREAM WITH BOURBON CARAMEL

Bourbon is made mostly from corn, so think of this dessert as a reunion of sweet corn, caramel, and bourbon. It highlights how a bourbon dessert can be savory and sweet at the same time. Enjoy this ice cream with a soft wheated bourbon, which you might even pour over the ice cream. Unlike your high school one, this is a reunion that you'll want to come back to again and again.

You'll need an ice cream maker to make this dessert. Any home model will work.

**Makes 1 quart ice cream and 6 cups caramel sauce**

**FOR THE ICE CREAM**

4 ears corn, shucked

4 cups heavy cream

1½ cups whole milk

8 large egg yolks

1¾ cups sugar

**FOR THE BROWN BUTTER BOURBON CARAMEL SAUCE**

3 cups sugar

¾ cup corn syrup

1 cup (2 sticks) unsalted butter

2½ cups heavy cream

¼ cup bourbon

1 teaspoon pure vanilla extract

½ teaspoon kosher salt

Ice cream cones, for serving (optional)

Preheat the oven to 375°F.

To make the ice cream, place the corn on a sheet pan and roast for 20 minutes, or until the ends of the cobs start to brown. Remove from the oven and let cool to room temperature.

Cut all the kernels from the cobs and place them in a large pot; add the cobs to the pot as well. Add the cream and milk and bring to a boil over high heat. Remove from the heat, cover with a lid, and steep for 40 minutes. Remove the corncobs and squeeze any liquid they've absorbed back into the pot, then discard the cobs. Transfer the contents of the pot to a blender and blend on high. Strain the corn milk mixture through a fine-mesh strainer set over the pot.

« CONTINUED »

In the bowl of a stand mixer fitted with the whisk attachment or in a large bowl using a handheld mixer, combine the egg yolks and sugar and whip on high speed until pale yellow and fluffy, about 3 minutes. Add 1 cup of the corn milk to the egg mixture and mix well. Pour the contents of the mixer bowl into the pot with the remaining corn milk.

Cook the corn mixture over medium heat, stirring continuously, until thickened, about 5 minutes. Remove from the heat and transfer the mixture to a bowl. Cover with plastic wrap, pressed directly against the surface to prevent a skin from forming, and chill the ice cream base in the fridge overnight.

The next day, churn the ice cream base in your ice cream maker according to the manufacturer's instructions.

While the ice cream is churning, make the brown butter bourbon caramel sauce: In a medium saucepan, combine ¾ cup water, the sugar, and the corn syrup and mix until combined. Cook over medium heat, without stirring, until the sugar begins to turn an amber color.

Meanwhile, in another pot, melt the butter over medium-high heat, then cook until the solids begin to brown, about 3 minutes. Turn off the heat and add the cream. Stir well and keep warm over low heat.

When the sugar in the first pan is a deep amber color, slowly add the warm cream mixture. It will bubble violently, so start with just a few spoonfuls, then you can slowly stream in the rest while whisking continuously. Don't worry if there are clumps of hard caramel; they will eventually melt. Reduce the heat to low and bring the caramel to a mild simmer. Cook for 2 to 3 minutes. Remove from the heat. Add the bourbon, vanilla, and salt and stir well, then transfer to a bowl and let cool completely.

When the ice cream is finished churning, transfer it to a large bowl and, using a wooden spoon, fold in some of the cooled bourbon caramel. Use as little or as much as you like in your ice cream, and save the rest for later. Place the ice cream in an airtight plastic container and freeze again for at least 1 hour before scooping into bowls (or cones, if using) and enjoying. The ice cream will keep in the freezer for up to 1 month.

# WESTERN KENTUCKY

On the western end of the bourbon trail, there are notable craft distilleries forging new paths and making great juice in the ever-evolving story of bourbon. The western part of the state is a bit less tamed, and the area's connection to moonshine is historic and well documented.

**DUELING GROUNDS DISTILLERY** got its name from the many disputes in this region that were settled by gunfight. Nowadays you can settle most matters by buying someone a round of drinks, and there's no better place to do that than at the bar at Dueling Grounds, where they make everything from four-year-old bourbon to gin to moonshine. There are farms everywhere in Western Kentucky, and **MB ROLAND DISTILLERY** makes a wonderful bourbon that uses their own locally grown white corn in the mash. The beauty of these small craft distillers is that they can source locally and be nimble with their products.

**CASEY JONES DISTILLERY** is named after the legendary pot still maker who rose to fame during the Prohibition era, and the facility is run by a family of the same lineage. **THE BARD DISTILLERY** was founded in 2015 by Thomas Bard, who is descended from William Bard, founder of Bardstown, Kentucky. Their distillery is housed in a hundred-year-old art deco former school building. They make Muhlenberg bourbon, which is the subject of a John Prine song. Play the song "Paradise" in your car on repeat on the drive, and you'll understand.

Similar to so many others, **GREEN RIVER DISTILLING CO.** was a historic and famed

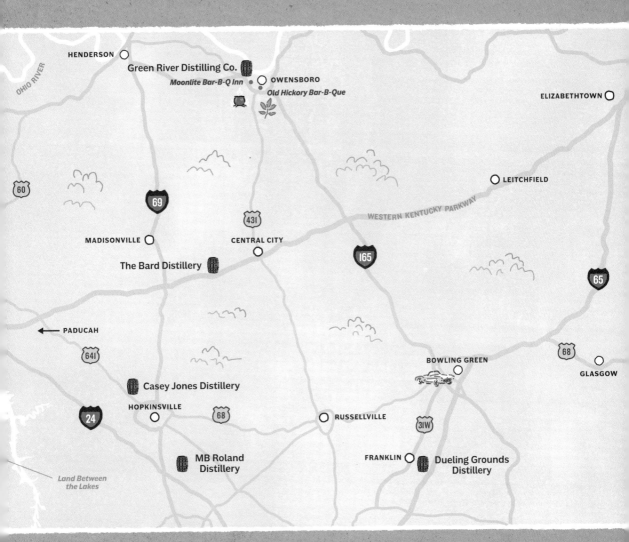

distillery founded by J. W. McCulloch in the late 1800s that fell victim to the mass distillery extinction during Prohibition. With much passion and determination, it has been revived. They make some incredibly rich bourbon, and though they're off the beaten path, I recommend a visit. Green River is located in the town of Owensboro, home to one of my favorite culinary delights: mutton barbecue. From the late 1800s until just before World War II, the wool industry was a prominent part of Kentucky's history, and mutton was plentiful. To this day, mutton barbecue is the backbone of two restaurant giants: Moonlite Bar-B-Q Inn and Old Hickory Bar-B-Que. I have a clear preference for one over the other, but I don't want to influence your vote, so you'll have to make the drive and decide for yourself.

# BOURBON'S ROAD AHEAD

According to the Kentucky Distillers' Association, there are nearly 10.5 million bourbon barrels aging in rickhouses across the state. Meanwhile, the population of Kentucky is roughly 4.4 million people. That means there are about two bourbon barrels aging in Kentucky for every human living in the state.

I've covered a lot in this book, and I hope the journey was insightful for you. But I've saved perhaps the most important aspect of this journey for last. Because this story is still very much unwritten. It is the story of diversity in bourbon.

It is not lost on me that I am a Korean American chef, born in Brooklyn, writing a book about Kentucky bourbon. The fact that I can even write a book on this subject and, what's more, have this book endorsed and embraced by so many, speaks volumes about Kentucky and, by extension, America.

As is common in American history, the contributions of people of color and Indigenous Americans were largely whitewashed out of the origin story of bourbon and of American whiskey as a whole. We'll never regain the part of that history, but we know several key ways in which their expertise and labor shaped the industry.

Corn is essential to bourbon, and regional Indigenous tribes, including the Cherokee, were adept at cultivating the crop. This farming by Indigenous Kentuckians, as well as their willingness, in many cases, to share what they knew with European settlers, enabled those settlers to farm corn on their own. In turn, farmers began distilling their excess corn into a very early form of bourbon.

In an episode of the radio project *The Next Louisville* titled "Where Are the Black People in Bourbon?" Patrick Lewis, a historian with the Kentucky Historical Society who specializes in the topics of slavery and the Civil War, states that historians know enslaved African Americans were involved with the early bourbon-making process, working on the farms and mills where bourbon was produced, but we don't know the full picture. Enslaved people weren't given a salary or compensation for the work they did, so slave owners didn't keep records of what work, exactly, they were doing. As a result, we have very little knowledge of who they were.

There have been efforts to rectify some of the lost histories of African American contributions to whiskey. In 2016, the *New York Times* published a story titled "Jack Daniel's Embraces a Hidden Ingredient: Help from a Slave." For many years, the whiskey lore presented the story of Jack Daniel as a basic apprentice story. When Daniel was a boy, he worked for a preacher/distiller named Reverend Dan Call, who taught the young boy everything about his unique method of charcoal distilling, known as the Lincoln County Process.

But the company now reports that Daniel actually learned the art of distillation from Nathan "Nearest" Green, one of the men Call had enslaved. Green was an admired distiller at the time, and when Call sold his distillery to Jack Daniel, Green was named Jack Daniel's first master distiller, which also made him the first African American master distiller in the United States. That may sound like an accomplishment worth celebrating, and Nathan Green did amass a good amount of wealth during his tenure with Jack Daniel's. But the sad truth is, he was never made partner or given proper credit for his role in the founding of this iconic whiskey brand, which means he never got his share of the incalculable profits that have created generational wealth for others.

As "Where Are the Black People in Bourbon?" reported, there are examples of credit given where credit is due in the history of Black bourbon. Tom Bullock was a Louisville-born bartender who became famous for his cocktails while working as a bartender at the St. Louis Country Club. He was the first African American person to write a cocktail book, called *The Ideal Bartender*, published in 1917. Bullock is credited with inventing the original old-fashioned cocktail during his stint at the Pendennis Club of Louisville (though some have claimed the recipe existed before the publication of Bullock's version). The book is still available today and has endured for generations, but if you read it, you'll notice that while Tom Bullock's name graces the cover, there is hardly any narrative about who Bullock was. This is also indicative of the history of the bartending world, where so many Black bartenders have been integral to the culture of pre-Prohibition cocktails but mostly erased from that history.

But as the world changes, so does bourbon. Bourbon marketing and advertising have become more diverse, and there seems to be an acknowledgment that BIPOC consumers will be the tastemakers guiding the future of bourbon. Kentucky finally has bourbon distilleries owned by Black makers, including Lexington's Fresh Bourbon (recognized by the state of Kentucky as the first African American–owned distillery to make Kentucky bourbon since slavery) and Brough Brothers Distillery in Louisville, which is making waves as a Black-owned luxury bourbon brand.

The climb toward diversity is not only one of race but also of gender. Increasingly, women are carving out their own space in the bourbon world. Samara Davis founded the Black Bourbon Society because she wanted to have an organization that advocated for diversity and inclusion in the spirits sector. As an avid bourbon fan, she created a space to drink bourbon with people who have felt excluded from the bourbon renaissance. Her membership is over thirty thousand strong and growing.

There is no doubt that the future of bourbon is going to be a collaborative effort. The list of women influencing bourbon is long, and they are creating the flavors and marketing campaigns and events and cocktails that will steer bourbon's popularity for the next generation. There are too many to name, but a few notable women in bourbon are Marianne Eaves, Kentucky's first female master distiller; Britt Kulsveen, president of Willett Distillery; Jane Bowie, director of innovation at Maker's Mark; Elizabeth McCall, master distiller at Woodford Reserve; Fawn Weaver, founder of Uncle Nearest Whiskey; and Jackie Zykan, former master taster at Old Forester.

When I sit down with the families that represent the lineage of historic bourbon, people like Fred Noe and Rob Samuels, they're thrilled to see the gospel of bourbon spreading globally. They understand that the future is diverse. They know that the popularity of bourbon (and its continued success) will be in the hands of bartenders of all races, creeds, religions, and opinions. We are the ones shaking the cocktails, spiking the punches, deglazing the sauces, serving the customers from Tokyo to London, São Paulo to Las Vegas, Melbourne to New Orleans. Bourbon started as Kentucky's finest spirit and has gone on to capture America's taste buds. It's only a matter of time before bourbon conquers the world.

But it all started in Kentucky, in a small corner of America that grew some corn, found some white oak, hammered out a copper still, captured some yeast, and waited patiently for the four seasons to do wonders with the barrel. Think about that the next time you open a bottle of bourbon. Close your eyes and taste all of it, all the history and the promising future, swirling around in your glass. Cheers!

# KENTUCKY DISTILLERIES

Before Prohibition, Kentucky boasted hundreds of distilleries throughout the state, but only six distilleries survived the period of Prohibition. Slowly, Kentucky has been building back the bourbon distillery business, and it is a vibrant part of the state's economy today. While we are not at pre-Prohibition numbers, there are plenty of Kentucky distilleries worth a visit on your next trip to Kentucky. Below is a list in alphabetical order.

**ANGEL'S ENVY DISTILLERY**
500 East Main Street, Louisville, KY

**AUGUSTA DISTILLERY**
207 Seminary Avenue, Augusta, KY

**BAKER-BIRD WINERY / B. BIRD DISTILLERY**
4465 Augusta Chatham Road, Augusta, KY

**THE BARD DISTILLERY**
5080 KY-175 South, Graham, KY

**THE BARDSTOWN BOURBON COMPANY**
1500 Parkway Drive, Bardstown, KY

**BARREL HOUSE DISTILLING CO.**
1200 Manchester Street, Lexington, KY

**BARTON 1792 DISTILLERY**
501 Cathedral Manor, Bardstown, KY

**BLUEGRASS DISTILLERS**
501 West 6th Street, #165, Lexington, KY

**BOONE COUNTY DISTILLING CO.**
10601 Toebben Drive, Florence, KY

**BOUNDARY OAK DISTILLERY**
2000 Boundary Oak Drive, Radcliff, KY

**BOURBON 30 SPIRITS DISTILLERY**
130 South Water Street, Georgetown, KY

**BROUGH BROTHERS DISTILLERY**
1460 Dixie Highway, Louisville, KY

**BUFFALO TRACE DISTILLERY**
113 Great Buffalo Trace, Frankfort, KY

**BULLEIT DISTILLING CO.**
3464 Benson Pike, Shelbyville, KY

**CASEY JONES DISTILLERY**
2815 Witty Lane, Hopkinsville, KY

**CASTLE & KEY DISTILLERY**
4445 McCracken Pike, Frankfort, KY

**COAL PICK DISTILLERY**
1825 Log Creek Lane, Drakesboro, KY

**DUELING BARRELS BREWERY & DISTILLERY**
745 Hambley Boulevard, Pikeville, KY

**DUELING GROUNDS DISTILLERY**
208 Harding Road, Franklin, KY

**EVAN WILLIAMS BOURBON EXPERIENCE**
528 West Main Street, Louisville, KY

**FOUR ROSES DISTILLERY**
1224 Bonds Mill Road, Lawrenceburg, KY

**GLENNS CREEK DISTILLING**
3501 McCracken Pike, Frankfort, KY

**GREEN RIVER DISTILLING CO.**
10 Distillery Road, Owensboro, KY

**HARTFIELD & CO. DISTILLERY**
320 Pleasant Street, Paris, KY

**HEAVEN HILL DISTILLERY**
1064 Loretto Road, Bardstown, KY

**HEAVEN'S DOOR DISTILLERY**
12606 Castle Highway, Pleasureville, KY

**JAMES E. PEPPER DISTILLERY**
1228 Manchester Street, #100, Lexington, KY

**JEPTHA CREED DISTILLERY**
500 Gordon Lane, Shelbyville, KY

**JIM BEAM AMERICAN OUTPOST**
568 Happy Hollow Road, Clermont, KY

**KENTUCKY ARTISAN DISTILLERY**
6230 Old Lagrange Road, Crestwood, KY

**KENTUCKY PEERLESS DISTILLING CO.**
120 North 10th Street, Louisville, KY

**LEXINGTON BREWING & DISTILLING CO.**
401 Cross Street, Lexington, KY

**LIMESTONE BRANCH DISTILLERY**
1280 Veterans Memorial Highway
Lebanon, KY

**LOG STILL DISTILLERY**
225 Dee Head Road, New Haven, KY

**LUX ROW DISTILLERS**
3050 East John Rowan Boulevard
Bardstown, KY

**MAKER'S MARK DISTILLERY**
3350 Burks Spring Road, Loretto, KY

**MB ROLAND DISTILLERY**
137 Barkers Mill Road, Pembroke, KY

**MICHTER'S DISTILLERY**
801 West Main Street, Louisville, KY

**NEELEY FAMILY DISTILLERY**
4360 KY-1130, Sparta, KY

**NEW RIFF DISTILLING**
24 Distillery Way, Newport, KY

**OLD BLUE RIBBON FARM**
2283 Ballardsville Road, Eminence, KY

**OLD FORESTER DISTILLING CO.**
119 West Main Street, Louisville, KY

**OLD POGUE DISTILLERY**
705 Germantown Road, Maysville, KY

**PAULEY HOLLOW DISTILLERY**
91 Kate Camp Branch, Forest Hills, KY

**PCS DISTILLING COMPANY**
436 Baxter Avenue, Louisville, KY

**RABBIT HOLE DISTILLERY**
711 East Jefferson Street, Louisville, KY

**REGENERATION DISTILLING CO.**
31 East Broadway Street, Winchester, KY

**ROUTE 52 DISTILLERY—KENTUCKY MOUNTAIN MOONSHINE**
465 Cow Creek, Irvine, KY

**SECOND SIGHT SPIRITS**
301 Elm Street, Ludlow, KY

**SILENT BRIGADE DISTILLERY**
426 Broadway Street, Paducah, KY

**TYLER WOOD DISTILLING COMPANY**
103 Whiskey Lane, Lewisburg, KY

**WHISKEY THIEF DISTILLING CO.**
283 Crab Orchard Road, Frankfort, KY

**WILDERNESS TRAIL DISTILLERY**
4095 Lebanon Road, Danville KY

**WILD TURKEY DISTILLERY**
1417 Versailles Road, Lawrenceburg, KY

**WILLETT DISTILLERY**
1869 Loretto Road, Bardstown, KY

**WOODFORD RESERVE DISTILLERY**
7785 McCracken Pike, Versailles, KY

# FURTHER READING

*American Whiskey, Bourbon & Rye: A Guide to the Nation's Favorite Spirit* by Clay Risen

*Barrel Strength Bourbon: The Explosive Growth of America's Whiskey* by Carla Harris Carlton

*The Big Book of Bourbon Cocktails* by Amy Zavatto

*The Bourbon Bible* by Eric Zandona

*The Bourbon Country Cookbook: New Southern Entertaining* by David Danielson and Tim Laird

*Bourbon Curious: A Simple Tasting Guide for the Savvy Drinker* by Fred Minnick

*Bourbon Empire: The Past and Future of America's Whiskey* by Reid Mitenbuler

*Bourbon Justice: How Whiskey Law Shaped America* by Brian F. Haara

*Bourbon: The Rise, Fall, and Rebirth of an American Whiskey* by Fred Minnick

*Bourbon: The Story of Kentucky Whiskey* by Clay Risen

*Bourbon, Straight: The Uncut and Unfiltered Story of American Whiskey* by Charles K. Cowdery

*Buffalo, Barrels, & Bourbon: The Story of How Buffalo Trace Distillery Became the World's Most Awarded Distillery* by F. Paul Pacult

*Kentucky Bourbon Country: The Essential Travel Guide* by Susan Reigler

*Kentucky Bourbon: The Early Years of Whiskeymaking* by Henry G. Crowgey

*The Kentucky Bourbon Experience: A Visual Tour of Kentucky's Bourbon Distilleries* by Leon Howlett

*Kentucky Bourbon Whiskey: An American Heritage* by Michael R. Veach

*Making Bourbon: A Geographical History of Distilling in Nineteenth-Century Kentucky* by Karl Raitz

*Pappyland: A Story of Family, Fine Bourbon, and the Things That Last* by Wright Thompson

*Straight Bourbon: Distilling the Industry's Heritage* by Carol Peachee

*Whiskey Lore's Travel Guide to Experiencing Kentucky Bourbon: Learn, Plan, Taste, Tour* by Drew Hannush

*Whiskey Women: The Untold Story of How Women Saved Bourbon, Scotch, and Irish Whiskey* by Fred Minnick

# ACKNOWLEDGMENTS

This book was not only a labor of love but a love letter to my Kentucky home. I am proud of the incredible talent from Kentucky that helped bring this book to life: Jessica Ebelhar, Rachel Sinclair, Susan Nguyen, Jeff Potter, Chris Bodden, and Ashlie Danielle Stevens. And a special shout-out to Dimity Jones, who is not from Kentucky, but we've drunk so much bourbon together that I consider you an honorary Kentuckian.

To my publishing family, who have always brought out the best in me—thank you, Judy Pray, Allison McGeehon, and Lia Ronnen.

To my agent, who has always been a beacon of sound advice—thank you, Kim Witherspoon.

To the team at 610 Magnolia, which has always been a model of patience and professionalism—I thank you.

To every distiller, bartender, whiskey writer, bourbon geek, and aficionado I have ever shared a drink with, this book is for you.

To my wife, Dianne, and my daughter, Arden, who are my daily inspirations to aspire to heights I would never have dreamed of by myself—thank you, and I love you with my whole heart.

# INDEX

# PHOTO CREDITS

**Page 23**: Kentucky Historical Society

**Pages 24–25**: 96PA101: James E. Pepper Company (bourbon whiskey distillery), Collection on Lafayette Studios, University of Kentucky Archives

**Page 26**: Kentucky Historical Society

**Page 44**: Science History Images/Alamy

**Page 47**: Shawshots/Alamy

**Page 109**: Kentucky Historical Society, Contributed by Harry Boone Nicholson Sr. to the Ohio River Portrait Project

**Page 149**: Old Visuals/Alamy

**Page 153**: zimmytws/Shutterstock.com

**Page 155**: BOS-49: Steamboat Congo, The Filson Historical Society, Louisville, KY

**Page 156**: Patti McConville/Alamy

**Page 158**: Kentucky Historical Society

**Page 159**: Patti McConville/Alamy

**Page 239**: Allstar Picture Library Ltd/Alamy

**Pages 240–241**: Pictorial Press Ltd/Alamy

**EDWARD LEE** is the chef/owner of 610 Magnolia and Nami in Louisville, Kentucky, and the culinary director for Succotash Restaurants in Washington, DC, and Maryland, for which he was awarded a Bib Gourmand from the Michelin Guide. He is also the cofounder of the LEE Initiative, a nonprofit dedicated to diversity and equality in the restaurant industry. He operates the nonprofit restaurant M. Frances in Washington, DC, as part of the LEE Initiative's overall mission. He was awarded the Muhammad Ali Humanitarian Award in 2021. Chef Lee was the recipient of the 2019 James Beard Foundation Award for his book *Buttermilk Graffiti: A Chef's Journey to Discover America's New Melting Pot Cuisine*. His first book was *Smoke & Pickles*. He was nominated for a Daytime Emmy for his role as host of the Emmy-winning PBS series *The Mind of a Chef*, and he has hosted and written a feature documentary called *Fermented*.